Ruthless

Second

Ruthless Execution

Second Edition

How Business Leaders Manage Through Turbulent Times

Amir Hartman
Craig LeGrande

Associate Publisher and Director of Marketing: Amy Neidlinger
Executive Editor: Jeanne Glasser Levine
Operations Specialist: Jodi Kemper
Cover Designer: Alan Clements
Managing Editor: Kristy Hart
Project Editor: Laura Hernandez
Copy Editor: Bart Reed
Proofreader: Debbie Williams
Indexer: Tim Wright
Compositor: Nonie Ratcliff
Manufacturing Buyer: Dan Uhrig

For information about buying this title in bulk quantities, or for special sales opportunities (which may include electronic versions; custom cover designs; and content particular to your business, training goals, marketing focus, or branding interests), please contact our corporate sales department at corpsales@pearsoned.com or (800) 382-3419.

For government sales inquiries, please contact governmentsales@pearsoned.com.

For questions about sales outside the U.S., please contact international@pearsoned.com.

Company and product names mentioned herein are the trademarks or registered trademarks of their respective owners.

Printed in the United States of America

First Printing September 2014

ISBN-10: 0-13-341077-3
ISBN-13: 978-0-13-341077-8

Pearson Education LTD.
Pearson Education Australia PTY, Limited.
Pearson Education Singapore, Pte. Ltd.
Pearson Education Asia, Ltd.
Pearson Education Canada, Ltd.
Pearson Educación de Mexico, S.A. de C.V.
Pearson Education—Japan
Pearson Education Malaysia, Pte. Ltd.

Library of Congress Control Number: 2014942464

Contents

Part III: Critical Capabilities

Foreword

When I joined IMS Health in 2000 as the CEO, I set ambitious goals for our business and challenged the executive team to look beyond the status quo to find new growth opportunities.

Our company was doing well but we had hit a "wall" in our effort to create further growth in our business. By increasing the company's investment in core data assets, analytics, and new product development, and dramatically strengthening the company's consulting and services capabilities, we were able to expand IMS Health into new markets and draw in new customers.

As an outcome of our management discipline, we were able to ramp up the company's pace of innovation and enhance IMS's global execution. But this did not mean that all went smoothly throughout my tenure. I think the adage is true that the most dangerous times for companies are when things are going well. There are no guarantees in business, and hitting performance walls can happen with very little warning. Leaders must persistently challenge their teams to innovate to avoid market pitfalls—and to accomplish this, business leaders must be focused on both setting a smart strategy and executing against it year-to-year.

Being able to make a quick, solid recovery from any bumps in the road was a skill that I found often goes unrecognized. That is why I have been delighted to read *Ruthless Execution* and to find that it offers a set of guidelines on how to avoid and manage through performance walls. As the book points out, leadership in today's marketplace requires continuous transformation. Breaking through performance walls is when one is truly tested. It's when the greatest pressure is put on the leadership team to deliver.

I like the way *Ruthless Execution* frames how leaders should develop a well-aligned set of strategic and portfolio management disciplines to ensure agility in the business. And how they can achieve new levels of customer loyalty and business performance through a reinvigorated focus on the customer and by communicating the true value of their company's products and services.

These simple and powerful frameworks—from strategy formulation to operational controls and corporate governance—offer business leaders a set of tried and true concepts to transform their own management practices. Of particular value is a new set of "critical capabilities" outlined in the book—customer success management and technology innovation—that provide thought-provoking models business leaders need to consider as they draw up their own strategic plans.

I've learned in my own business career that success is driven by a cogent strategic vision, simply communicated, managed continuously, and paired with strong incentives to ensure successful execution.

The true value of this book is in giving executives an understanding of what it means to engage in ruthless execution in today's turbulent economic times. The message of the book is simply this: Hitting a performance wall is inevitable. But as this book so wisely points out, we as leaders can effectively leap over these walls with the right leadership practices in place.

—David Thomas, former CEO of IMS Health and
chairman of Fortune Brands, July 2014

Acknowledgments

In our 25 years working for and advising some of most admired companies and business leaders, we have had the privilege of rubbing shoulders with many business leaders who served to enrich our understanding of the business world.

We want to particularly thank Patty Morrison, Debbie Mitchell, and Eileen Lehmann from Cardinal Health; Jeb Dasteel and Carol Sato from the Oracle Corporation; Tony Ueber and the folks at Banfield; and Sujeet Chand at Rockwell Automation. These are leaders who not only helped us get a better handle on key concepts in the book, but also showed how the leadership practices manifest themselves within their organizations. These executives took time away from their busy days to sit down with us to talk about their experiences. We want to particularly acknowledge Dave Thomas, former CEO of IMS Health and chairman of Fortune Brands, for honoring us with the Foreword to this book, and sharing with us how he has managed through turbulent times.

Also contributing to our development of key concepts in this book are Bryan Tantzen and Amal Radia from Cisco, Nick Mehta from Gainsight, and Matt Stein from GE.

We want to express our sincere gratitude to Rob Bracken for some crucial advice and the time he gave in shaping the structure and writing of this book. We also want to thank our colleagues at Mainstay—not only for their encouragement, but for their input on many topics. Lastly, thanks go out to our families, who often feel the burden of such a project the most. We are truly grateful for their support.

About the Authors

An authority on corporate and technology transformations, **Amir Hartman** is an international bestselling author and advisor to leading global businesses. Hartman has been on the faculty at Columbia's Graduate School of Business, Berkeley's Haas School of Business, and Harvard Business School Interactive where he's taught management of innovation and technology to senior business leaders. A frequent speaker at business leader forums, he is the author of several influential books, most recently *Ruthless Execution: How Business Leaders Manage Through Turbulent Times*. Prior to forming Mainstay, Mr. Hartman served as managing director for Cisco System's Corporate Internet Strategy and the Internet Business Solutions Group. In this role he was responsible for shaping Cisco's Internet business strategy and advising key customers on Internet business strategies.

Craig LeGrande has served as senior advisor to leading companies in the automotive, retail, and high-technology industries, helping them identify new market opportunities and develop effective capital investment strategies. The author of more than a hundred case studies and research papers for high-technology leaders such as Oracle, SAP, EDS, BearingPoint, EMC, and Network Appliance, Mr. LeGrande is an expert at proving business value by means of objective, quantitative evidence and analysis. Prior to forming Mainstay, Mr. LeGrande worked in Cisco's Internet Business Solutions Group and Accenture's Strategic Services group. He received an MBA from the Tuck School of Business at Dartmouth College and a BS in Electrical Engineering with Honors.

Part I
Managing Through Tough Times

1

Introduction to Ruthless Execution

Ruthless execution is the term we use for the methods and strategies business leaders employ to break through performance walls and manage through turbulent times. We first employed this term in 1996 when we were doing work for Hewlett-Packard (HP). During the research process for this and our first *Ruthless* book, it became clear that the same term captured the essence of the strategies that business leaders execute to overcome tough or turbulent times.

Few books have focused on how companies navigate tough times and how these same companies have come back stronger and more nimble from that experience. Books on American corporate life have tended to proffer advice on how to steer a business during good or "normal" times. As we've witnessed over the past decade plus, leaders are realizing they need to plan for more of a roller coaster ride than a rocket ship. A new fact of life in business has become clear: Invariably, business leaders are going to experience tough or turbulent times. Accordingly, this book tries to prepare companies for taking advantage of the "ups" as well as offers practical ways to build corporate resilience to manage through the "downs."

Hitting a Performance Wall

We define **hitting the performance wall** as a rude awakening that occurs when a company has enjoyed consistent high-level performance and then experiences two or more years of flat or declining growth. This flat performance can be driven by different factors: a downward turn in the economy, a lack of product innovation, growth that occurs too rapidly, a missed market opportunity, or, as is most often the case, ineffective execution. The awakening is typically "rude" because most business leaders don't see it coming, and it is often preceded by strong performance.

In this book, there is no attempt to explain why companies hit a performance wall. That sort of analysis has been the subject of a number of other books and articles. More important to note is that what causes reversals is most often controllable. Irrespective of cause, almost always it is an inability to focus and execute that is at the heart of the problem.

Indeed, if hitting a wall has become a new business norm, if the potential for a business reversal haunts the leadership of companies more now than at any other time, it makes sense to offer urgent guidance on how to navigate a path of success, or how to recover after *hitting the wall.*

From 2000 to 2003, we investigated companies in this predicament, companies that over the long run had been strong performers, but from time to time had fallen into periods of stagnation. From our research, we came up with a way of looking at these companies that we found extremely useful.

The long and the short is that it's becoming more and more difficult to be a successful business leader. Given the quickened pace of change in the last few decades—changes wrought by major waves of technology innovation, sharper competition, empowered customers, and "smart" products—the business environment is confusing, complex, and uncertain.

A way forward exists that requires doing nothing more than studying business leaders who have gotten themselves through these difficult situations. *The leaders who have pulled themselves through these tough times share certain behavioral patterns, exhibiting "ruthless execution."*

In 2000, watching companies struggle with the collapse of the "New Economy" and ensuing economic downturn, we became interested in uncovering the ingredients that leaders who overcame these struggles shared. That became the thrust of three years of research, which eventually made it clear that *the notion of ruthless execution could serve well as a powerful and overarching framework for guiding business leaders through turbulent times and performance uncertainties that inevitably occur.*

The research examined companies that had at one time or another suffered setbacks. The goal was to discover what practices these companies employed that helped them break through the performance walls and manage through these times. The means was to study a diverse set of industries and companies, large and small, using surveys, company documents, research reports, publicly available financial data (10-Ks), and, where possible, interviews with key business leaders. At times, we served as a consultant to these companies, enabling us to build case studies of these enterprises.

What we learned is that ruthless execution means that business leaders take the time and opportunity to study the issues—and then act on them. During tough times, leaders do not have to rush into making decisions, but just the opposite. They have predefined strategic and operational methodologies that allow them to uncover issues early and react prudently, focusing the company's efforts to drive through the wall. Indeed, business leaders who have broken through performance walls have tended to be very fact based, team oriented, and analytical in their approach to problem solving.

Exhibiting patience is a definite requirement for making decisions in uncertain times, because the last thing you want to do is to suggest that it is easy to revitalize an organization.

To be clear, this book is not about fixing companies in crisis. This book is about learning from leaders who were able to manage through the turbulent times and perform again. The plain truth is that most large corporations—more than 90 percent of all public companies— suffer rude awakenings from time to time; indeed, setbacks happen to these large enterprises frequently. Large, established companies can become complacent; they may become too bureaucratic to innovate. Also, innovative enterprises may favor hyper-growth at the expense of discipline and rigor.

To highlight the challenges of consistent performance in these turbulent times, we researched the financial performance of the Fortune 500 over a 12-year period (2001-2012), removing the Great Recession years of 2008-2010 given the exceptional challenges of these years. Over this period, not a single company in the Fortune 500 had consecutive years of revenue and profit growth. Lowering the bar even further, only 3 companies were able to achieve revenue and profit growth for all except 2 years during this period.

Ruthless Execution II

As was the case with the first edition of *Ruthless,* the strategies of ruthless execution are framed in three distinct categories that are already part and parcel of every executive's daily life: *leadership, critical capabilities, and governance.* After a decade of turbulent times in which businesses faced down a great recession and made it through, we wanted to see whether the *Ruthless* concepts were still valid. Did companies who were able to weather the storm employ some of the same strategies? Were new approaches born in the process? Within each of these categories, a number of practices will be detailed throughout the book. What we've tried to do with the new edition is validate what still holds true more than a decade later and, more important, document what's new or different from the previous strategies employed. There is no suggestion that engaging successfully in any one of these strategies automatically allows you to break through a performance wall. The idea is to point out the common ingredients and practices of business leaders who have figured out how to effectively manage through turbulent times.

Leadership

Leadership frames the specific actions that drive strategic recalibration from formulation to execution, and to a degree, the characteristics that business leaders need to overcome business reversals. The focus in the leadership category is on strategic formulation.

The key questions to answer for this category are as follows:

- What is important to your company? How do you fundamentally create value?
- What is your "return on strategy"? Are you effectively balancing between performance-oriented initiatives and growth efforts?
- Has a clear focus been defined and effectively communicated throughout the organization?

What has emerged in the past decade is that rather than this being an exercise that leaders do every three years as part of their long-range planning, today's *Ruthless* leaders employ these concepts on an ongoing basis. The best organizations are continuously undergoing transformational efforts.

After developing necessary strategies, business leaders are ready for the actual recalibration process to occur. They must put in place a number of critical capabilities that are, in and of themselves, the very essence of recalibrating.

Critical Capabilities

Critical capabilities are the specific initiatives that executives must make part of the corporate DNA in order to survive the tectonic shifts in today's markets. Critical capabilities are very action oriented. As was the case more than a decade ago, these critical capabilities include productivity management, talent management, and focused corporate transactions (mergers, acquisitions, and divestitures). However, two new critical capabilities have emerged: managing customer success and what we call the "cloudification" of business. It is through these critical capabilities that business leaders can leap over their competition and clear current performance hurdles.

The key questions to answer for this category are as follows:

- Are costs and productivity improvements in the DNA of the organization?
- How good are you at finding and getting rid of nonperformers?
- What business functions should you keep and which should you let go?
- What measurable value are your customers harvesting from your products/solutions?
- How is the cloud and Big Data changing the way you deliver value to customers?

Governance

Governance spells out the rules of the game; it deals with issues such as the way decisions get made and the discipline that leaders impose on their teams. Toward that end, leaders need to operate within the governance framework, with accountability, performance management, and discipline as the main strategic drivers for determining how to engage in the recalibration process.

The key questions to answer for this category are as follows:

- Do you have a disciplined process for allocating resources and spending capital?

- Do you use the right performance measures, and are you measuring the right things?

- Do you have a disciplined performance-management process in place?

- Are Big Data and the cloudification of business on the board's agenda?

- Does the board meet regularly with customers to understand the value they are delivering?

Throughout this book, case studies will be used to illustrate a particular ruthless execution strategy. These studies show how the company in question has used one or more of the strategies to cope. We believe that you also can benefit by employing one strategy or another in your own efforts to manage through turbulent times and break through your performance walls.

Lastly, we introduce the Ruthless Execution Index. This index can serve as a "signpost" for business leaders who want to understand where they can improve their ruthless execution. We encourage you to revisit these practices on a regular basis.

Part II
Leadership

2

Strategic Recalibration and the Business Philosophy

You've got to eat while you dream. You've got to deliver on short-range commitments while you develop a long-range strategy and vision and implement it. The success of doing both. Walking and chewing gum if you will. Getting it done in the short range, and delivering a long-range plan and executing on that.

—Jack Welch

The Ruthless Execution Checklist

- Are we better at what matters to our customers?
- Which strategic battlefields must we win?
- Are we spending the right amount in the right areas to win these battlefields?
- Have we aligned resources to maximize our chances for success?
- Are we holding people accountable for results?

As noted in Chapter 1, "Introduction to Ruthless Execution," leadership frames the specific actions that drive strategic formulations—and to a degree, the characteristics that key leaders need to overcome business reversals.

The term **leadership** is so common within the business framework that it almost seems unnecessary to define it. To make matters a bit more complicated, leadership can highlight many different things. However, we want to highlight the specific aspects of leadership that are critical to ruthless execution: strategic recalibration, the ardent commitment to translating strategy to an executable plan, consistent and periodic reviews of progress against the plan, and incentives and consequences for those tasked with managing execution.

Our experience with large enterprises has found a wide disparity of effectiveness in developing winning business strategies. As one large automobile manufacturer executive once mentioned to us, "If I stacked up all the management consulting engagements we've had to fix our supply chain, I could fill up my office from floor to ceiling"—and he had a very large office. What causes these failures? Often it's the inability to create strategies that are executable. As was the case for the auto manufacturer, great ideas may not be practical to implement.

After seeing the good, the bad, and the ugly of business strategic-planning processes and their too frequent failures in execution, we began to formulate ideas on how to create a more effective strategy-to-execution process, one that creates a very simple blueprint for a diverse team of people to follow to maximize the prospects for success. As you'll read later in this chapter, leadership needs to be steadfast in keeping focused on a few major bets and not falling into the "thousand flowers bloom" approach. They must also be relentless in monitoring and managing the programs and projects that execute against this plan. It is these reviews of the accomplishments and failures experienced annually that feed back into the next year's recalibration of the strategic plan and the reprioritization of projects in which the company invests its capital.

Strategic Recalibration

As we discussed in Chapter 1, one of the things that has changed in the past decade is the concept of strategy. Whereas in the past, the strategy-formulation and strategic transformation processes were done every three to five years, today we are finding that the best companies are undergoing these processes on an ongoing basis. Leaders now are constantly reviewing and testing their core business, assessing market changes and the competitive landscape. By ensuring the company is maximizing new opportunities, avoiding market pitfalls, and meeting changing customer needs, these leaders can be confident they are optimally deploying the people, capital, and other assets of the company.

Strategic recalibration, simply put, is the act of validating the direction a company is going to take and focusing on that direction. As companies attempt to validate that direction, they realign and reconfigure their resources so that they are balancing between performance-driven and growth-driven initiatives.

Business leaders over the past decade (2003–2013) were likely anticipating the duration of the recession and its magnitude. Even in the past two years, with clear evidence that the recession is past us, companies have remained slow to hire and allocate resources. How companies pared expenses without killing the good with the bad was essential to navigating through these turbulent times.

Despite the real need for most business leaders to recalibrate their business strategies and corresponding project portfolios, very few companies have an established method for such an effort. A lack of process around this can often exacerbate a company's poor performance, and a lack of a unifying measure can make prioritization decisions difficult and political in nature. Because biases and politics tend to shape these decisions and actions, they can often lead to an executive's mistaken belief that most products, services, and customers are strategically critical, when in reality few are.

In this chapter, we focus on the strategy-formulation process and the need to revisit often "passed-down" processes that are out of date. Our experience in working with some of the largest and most well-known global companies is that these processes have often been culturally embedded in their organizations and are managed by the "chosen few" strategic people in the company. The strategy process is often viewed as a "necessary evil" by the operators of the business, the business line executives, to win budget approvals for their projects. In today's accelerated business environment, these legacy processes are now outdated. With the ever-increasing pace of technical innovations and the subsequent breakdown of traditional industry barriers, the ability to anticipate change and act nimbly to stay ahead of competition starts and ends with strategic recalibration.

In this chapter, we explore how best-of-breed companies are managing their corporate strategy process. We'll then discuss in Chapter 3, "Portfolio Management Discipline," how to implement an execution engine to ensure your company meets its strategic goals.

Why do some companies seem to outflank or outpace their competition? What leadership actions have these companies taken? Our research sheds light on a common problem that starts in the boardroom, with directors unable to look at new, innovative ways to transform their industries, and who are often shutting out key executives who could help to shape the company's direction. As a well-respected CEO, now a Fortune 100 board director, told us, "Directors listening to CIOs are like dogs watching TV"—they listen but they don't understand. In fact, we found that out of the 100 plus Fortune 500 boards we studied, only 1 percent of these directors had a background in science, technology, engineering, or math (STEM).

The lack of technical acumen on boards can cause what a former chief technology officer and Fortune 500 board member stated was a shortage in "cognitive diversity," thus hindering creative thinking and leaving CIOs with little opportunity to influence business direction.

This lack of diversity also cascades down to executive management. Just a few years ago, a global study found that 59 percent of non-IT management did not believe that IT's contribution to innovation was important to their companies. These same companies did not measure IT's impact and mostly viewed these departments as back-office support functions.

With the rise of cloud-enabled business opportunities and social media, never has technology played a more important role in shaping the competitive landscape. As we'll discuss in a later section of the book, new critical capabilities around the cloud and customer success management will be keys to growing and staying profitable in the years ahead. Corporate board members' ability to help guide and orchestrate their company's adoption and mastery of these new critical capabilities will require an understanding of the underlying technical requirements and implications. The question for you is, Is your board equipped for the challenges of today's marketplace?

The leaders we studied were able to design a strategic recalibration process that provided the board with a blueprint for how the company could capture the new opportunities presented by the cloud and customer centricity. We have found from our work with leading global organizations that this process offers a powerful communication vehicle that can help align the entire organization, from the board to the mailroom.

Revitalizing the Core

Effective leaders understand that a company, after hitting a performance wall, must try to revitalize its core businesses and not wander off the path into diversified ventures that do not play to its core capabilities.

But how does one do those things? Companies must start by focusing on stabilizing and revitalizing their core revenues. The enticements to enter new markets are often out there and are hard to overcome. As markets expand, every company wants to get a large share of those markets. Also, some companies that are doing well in one market conclude that they understand the principles of business well enough to migrate into other markets without asking whether they have that right. This is especially true of companies that have a strong cash position.

Good leaders know that a wise course of action is to take a good, hard look at their best customers and build new capabilities to stay closer to them. After all, these were the people who made their businesses a success at one point—and they can do it again. These customers may want different products, services, or approaches to partnering to meet their future needs; they may want better prices, new pricing strategies, or a shift in ownership of business processes (for instance, a cloud-based business process instead of on-premises). Regardless of what they want, they were at one time the business' best customers. A key act of recalibration would be to understand the changes to the business model that will regain their trust and support and make them a focus of the business once again.

These same successful leaders also appreciate that engaging in strategic recalibration needs to be a recurring process, in both good times and bad. Some of the best business minds have used dismal economic periods to get a jump on the competition whereas others have outpaced the competition to identify shifts in customer demand and grab new market opportunities.

Steve Jobs' vision and relentless focus on new, innovative products turned a near-dead company into the most valued company on the planet; Alan Mulally's ability to refocus Ford on rebuilding its core brands was instrumental to turning the corner for the iconic auto manufacturer. Jeff Bezos' Amazon continues to grow through investments in technology-enabled offshoots of its core online retailing operation, such as IT infrastructure services.

Reading the Environment

Reading the environment correctly is crucial when engaging in strategic recalibration. No time in recent history has this been more important than the past 14 years. With economic conditions hitting a wall in 2001 after the Internet bubble collapse, then again in the wake of the financial crisis of 2008, leaders continue to face extraordinary market turbulence and remain understandably wary even today.

Fresh challenges in reading the environment are complicating leaders' efforts to strategically recalibrate. Factors such as environmental activism, healthcare reform, currency fluctuations, yield curve manipulation, and government stimulus all create macroeconomic uncertainties that can make capital investment decisions truly perplexing.

The time pressures for business leaders to break through performance walls continue to shorten in the current century because of the heightened media attention, the plethora of social media and cable news outlets, and the increasing voice and influence of Wall Street activists.

As a recent example, look at the challenges that John Donahoe has faced since taking the helm at eBay. This iconic technology brand has faced continued scrutiny over not spinning off its PayPal business unit, even though its market value has jumped by 60 percent since 2008 and revenue at the unit has been growing at 27 percent a year. When corporate activists such as Carl Icahn take on even well-performing companies, the CEO must be prepared to articulate a sound strategy to combat these outside forces. We're happy to note that as of the writing of this book, Mr. Donahoe had done just that, demonstrating a sound plan for keeping PayPal a part of eBay.

Guidelines for Strategic Recalibration

We've presented the case for why companies need a strong strategic recalibration process. Now we would like to introduce you to a proven approach to that process that we've implemented for our global clients. We will also present a customer case example of the impact a sound strategic process can have on an organization. Our work with Cardinal Health, a leader in the healthcare industry, found that a focus on constant reinvention of its business has been a critical factor in the Fortune 500 company's success.

Our goal in the remainder of this chapter is to present our approach with a step-by-step guide to strategic recalibration.

Strategic Recalibration—Where to Start?

In our work helping Fortune 500 organizations, we have found that most strategic plans are led by the chief financial officer, and often are, at best, a loosely affiliated appendage to the annual budgeting process. In fact, a successful annual plan is dependent on a well-crafted and focused strategic plan. The "thousand flowers bloom" strategy needs to be thrown into the trash heap of business management theory. The thousand flowers bloom strategy refers to the approach of investing in many projects with the hope that one or a few will "bloom" or bear fruit. The issue with this approach is that it often creates projects whereby too few resources and attention are dedicated, they are underfunded, they lack the management attention to succeed, and they often peter out with little to show for themselves, creating confusion and indecision across the company.

The time has come for executive leaders to abandon micromanaging the annual budget and shift to creating and coordinating a truly effective strategic plan. For example, we know of a $16 billion Fortune 500 company that spent six weeks developing the company's strategic plan with a small team of internally hired, junior-level ex-management consultants. The output of the effort was only half-heartedly accepted by the executive team and, behind closed doors, was viewed as a "necessary evil" to meet the corporate board's requirements. The exercise was more theoretical than practical.

Meanwhile, the executive team was preoccupied with the annual financial planning process, which took six months and was rife with haggling and internal infighting for budget dollars. The pennywise-pound-foolish approach to planning meant that major strategic opportunities were missed, smaller "pet projects" were approved, and bickering groups lacked the coordination to successfully attack new competitive opportunities. It was no surprise that the company stagnated.

What this company failed to do—and what a strong strategic plan requires—is to take the time to build consensus around a vision for the company, creating in the process a cohesive set of top initiatives for the business. In fact, we have found that 99 percent of innovative ideas already exist within the management team of the business. Sadly, though, the political and bureaucratic culture of companies causes most of these ideas to be either missed or squashed.

To capture innovation and build actionable programs, we've crafted the Strategic Alignment and Recalibration (STAR) process (see Figure 2-1). The goals of the STAR process are as follows:

- Align the entire executive team and board of directors behind a two-to-three-year strategic vision for the company.
- Create a framework to communicate simply and effectively the vision, key objectives, critical programs, and expected results of the two-year plan.
- Build milestones, checkpoints, and adjustment mechanisms into the plan to ensure the necessary flexibility to manage the business effectively.

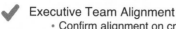 Executive Team Alignment
   • Confirm alignment on critical business outcomes

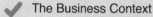 The Business Context
   • Assess the business challenges facing XXXX and align the key players on the specific 3 YR priorities and challenges

 START – Business Outcomes Model
   • Gain clarity on XXXXX strategic initiatives, and the supporting measurable business outcomes, including specific process operating model implications and underlying technology enablement required.

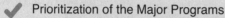 Prioritization of the Major Programs
   • Gain consensus on the top business program opportunities with a focus on the first 180 days, or first project(s) associated with these programs

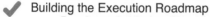 Building the Execution Roadmap
   • Develop a detailed profile of the major activities required for each of the top project opportunities, key sponsors and skill requirements, risks and key milestones to ensure success

Figure 2-1   Objectives of the STAR process

The STAR Process

The STAR process has three major phases: from vision to strategic initiatives, from strategic initiatives to process implications, and from process implications to technology implications. In our experience, the first phase is the most critical and is best run in a facilitated workshop setting. The goal here is to clearly articulate what you are, and will be, for your customers, employees, shareholders, and partners. Once this is developed, a gap analysis of what needs to be accomplished to reach this goal should be developed. We've found that this process can lead to a number of strategic battlefields—these are key areas in the marketplace that you must win. However, management must show discipline by culling the list of targets to a select few (about three to five) to ensure the proper attention and resources can be organized behind the effort.

The number of workshops, participants, and supporting resources will need to be customized to your company's size and structure, but best practice would require for this process to be reviewed and updated annually.

The second phase is the development of strategic initiatives. These are the keys to winning a particular battlefield. Start with a high-level goal for each initiative and then define a specific set of business outcomes that determine success for each one. This process can be assigned to different work teams that ultimately will own each initiative.

It is very important when defining an initiative to understand how it can impact existing business processes and what critical operational changes will be needed to meet the initiative's goals. In our experience, the hardest initiatives to launch are those that involve synchronizing different business units and functional departments.

The third phase is to identify how the strategic process changes will impact the company's current technology programs and investments. This is a critical step to ensure that new processes are fully automated to reach their maximum potential.

The STAR strategic blueprint—ideally a one-page document—can be the single most important tool for communicating a company's strategic realignment to the company—from the board to the entry-level employee. On a single page, the blueprint outlines the critical direction, efforts, requirements, and outcomes to align a company for long-term success (see Figure 2-2). The document also serves as a critical input for the portfolio-management process, which takes the strategic plan and details the execution approach for the company. In short, the STAR strategic blueprint highlights the "big bets" that form the heart of the company's project portfolio.

Leaders use the STAR process as a practical tool to help prioritize their projects and investment portfolios. We've found that portfolio planning has made significant strides over the past decade, with more companies establishing program and portfolio management offices and deploying automated planning and tracking tools. Our point here is to encourage companies to more closely align their strategy development effort, through the STAR process, with the portfolio management and annual budgeting process.

Vision	What makes our company unique and valuable to our customers?			
Strategic Initiatives	What 2-3 year program will drive reaching our vision?	What 2-3 year program will drive reaching our vision?	What 2-3 year program will drive reaching our vision?	What 2-3 year program will drive reaching our vision?
	How do we measure the financial success of the program?	How do we measure the financial success of the program?	How do we measure the financial success of the program?	How do we measure the financial success of the program?
Business Outcomes	Are there specific operational checkpoints along the way?	Are there specific operational checkpoints along the way?	Are there specific operational checkpoints along the way?	Are there specific operational checkpoints along the way?
	What are the strategic measures of success?	What are the strategic measures of success?	What are the strategic measures of success?	What are the strategic measures of success?
	What are the operational measures of success?	What are the operational measures of success?	What are the operational measures of success?	What are the operational measures of success?
Process Implications	What are functional processes that require change?		What are functional processes that require change?	
	Are there any organizational impacts?		Are there any organizational impacts?	
	Do we need any outside expertise?		Do we need any outside expertise?	
	How do we best communicate with suppliers & vendors?		How do we best communicate with suppliers & vendors?	
	How do we best market our new capabilities to customers/the market?		How do we best market our new capabilities to customers/the market?	
Technology Implications	Application Requirements/Capabilities		Technical Resource Alignment	
	Infrastructure Requirements/Capabilities		IT Partner/Vendor Management	
	Information Security			

Figure 2-2 The STAR blueprint

Many companies think in terms of portfolios of businesses. This made sense in the heady days of the late 1990s, when managing a business for hyper-growth was a focus. But managing through the turbulent times of the past decade and revitalizing an organization organically takes a lot more focus. This is the goal of portfolio management (see Figure 2-3).

A critical step for business leaders in executing business strategies is to rearrange their portfolios of business initiatives—the set of projects, investments, and other efforts that their businesses are working on and allocating resources and attention to carry out.

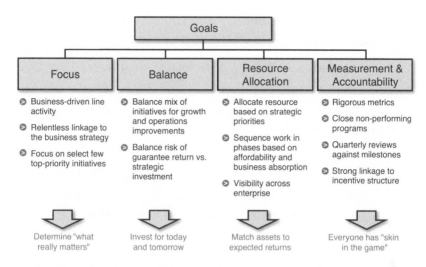

Figure 2-3   The goals of recalibration

Recalibrating by adopting a portfolio-of-initiatives strategy encourages executives to be more flexible, immediate, and action oriented. The very notion of strategic recalibration is to monitor circumstances, to engage in rigorous analysis of each initiative, and to adapt to changing circumstances. There is ample opportunity to alter initiatives in mid-course, which is a great plus. We will go into detail on the concept of portfolio management in the next chapter.

The Business Philosophy—Communicating the Journey

What is meant by a business philosophy? A **business philosophy** is a set of guidelines or directives that helps leaders communicate and institutionalize what's important to their businesses. Business leaders establish these guidelines, which form a basic ingredient of a company's culture, to help colleagues run their businesses. Business philosophies are useful for executives who are struggling with what steps to take to break through walls. Business leaders who have successfully overcome reversals rely on business philosophies that embrace all the ingredients of *ruthless execution*.

Business philosophies emanate from the top; they are highly individualistic, and they tend to be identified with the head of a company.

It is frequently said that great companies require great cultures, but the features that comprise company cultures are often vague and fuzzy, and are far too general to provide employees with operational roadmaps. In fact, organizational culture can often be an inhibiting factor for change and renewal. It can breed inertia and a sense of complacency. Instead, what is needed to manage though tough times is focus, action, and doing things differently. On the other hand, a *business philosophy,* if tightly scripted and highly delineated, offers clear guidance to employees.

A business philosophy is specific and deals with practical, everyday issues. Because cultural elements tend to be unspecific, it is that much more difficult for executives to get past business reversals by adhering to those elements. Instead, by listening to a leader articulate a business philosophy, executives have a far more focused and delineated roadmap for how to behave.

Executives who take the time to put together a coherent, tightly scripted business philosophy and communication roadmap are going to be able to energize and motivate their employees at a time when they are typically less motivated, during a period of struggle and stagnation. The benefits of putting together a business philosophy should be self-evident. A business philosophy provides meaning to the strategies and goals of a company, making them easier to understand and therefore easier to implement. The business philosophy provides clear "signposts" to employees, explaining to them how things should truly be—and, of critical importance, it helps create a sense of energy that will help to achieve the strategies and goals. The crucial benefit of the business philosophy is to help everyone place the emphasis on doing the right things rather than doing things right. Emphasizing doing the right things is another way of talking about strategic recalibration: It is figuring out where the company should be focusing, as opposed to doing a lot of things that effectively fall outside that focus.

The absence of a business philosophy is a prescription for chaos, lack of focus, and inefficiency. An effective business philosophy helps get employees to understand what is important to the company and what is not.

The best business philosophies contain certain "universal" elements: Business leaders make sure that everyone strives to get jobs done—to ruthlessly execute. They set priorities and take actions based on those priorities.

Once a business philosophy is created, executives display a set of traits that reflects how they manage inline with that business philosophy. These leaders of the *ruthless execution* school are decisive, but impersonal, no-nonsense and cerebral, and very demanding. In short, they know how to drive discipline within their companies.

They display a healthy, introspective attitude toward their companies. They evaluate the health of their companies objectively, assessing where their companies' strengths and weaknesses lie. They try to avoid falling into the trap of simply blaming external factors for their companies' setbacks. They are very fact based.

Perhaps the greatest value of *ruthless execution* is helping business leaders determine whether their companies are simply in difficult times or in crisis. Mostly, these leaders find that their companies have fallen within a period of uncertainty, and they search for business philosophies appropriate for such times. Realizing that, they can understand that it makes little sense to take drastic action (across-the-board layoffs, for example) or to change long-range strategic visions. Rather, they require a business philosophy that is sensible, demanding, and disciplined.

Such a cool-headed, detached approach permits these leaders to deal more selectively with various ways to break through walls. Engaging in *ruthless execution,* in short, means not acting suddenly or randomly; it means not simply taking across-the-board actions; it means taking into account the differences that exist within a company.

The Six-Month Shuffle

When leaders don't know what is really driving their poor performance, they invoke the "two quarter rule" for recovery. It is an innocuous statement to the analyst community that things will improve in six months, thus buying them some time to figure things out and enough time for the analysts to forget the rule was involved in the first place.

Those leaders who really understand the value of creating a business philosophy communicate it relentlessly, with targeted messages to all constituents (employees, management team, shareholders, and so on). Most important, they live by very clear rules when it comes to communicating with their constituents:

- **Straight talk**—The rule here is to have only clear and honest discussions on what the company needs to get done and what is expected of people. The rule insists that everyone face and understand the reality of the situation.

- **No surprises**—Here, the rule is to be consistent, to make sure everyone is on the same page. It means being very clear about the focus and key battlefields that the business needs to take on. It means setting very clear expectations, being up front with everyone. It means being clear about what needs to be done by not concealing important issues but rather putting them front and center.

- **Just the facts**—This rule argues against getting emotional about assessing the situation and communicating actions. The discussion here should include evidence, including numbers, about why you want to go in one direction as opposed to another. There should be facts behind the message.

- **Keep promises**—It's not enough to talk straight, to be consistent, and to give the facts. You've got to deliver. You've got to do what you say you are going to do. If you don't, nothing else you say (or do) will matter.

Communicating Consistently

Being able to communicate regularly and consistently to stakeholders is at the heart of any business philosophy. A business leader who says one thing one day and another the next confuses employees as well as produces a negative effect on shareholders and Wall Street—two institutions that no one wants to embitter. With a purpose of uniting the company behind a clear-cut goal, the business philosophy has less of the feel of a vision and more the sense of a rallying cry for short-term action.

In articulating a business philosophy, a business leader acts more like a cheerleader than a business executive. Being a cheerleader does not automatically mean a business leader is charismatic or charming, although at times a Jeff Bezos, Steve Jobs, Larry Ellison, or John Chambers does come along. Most business leaders are just ho-hum speakers, but some of the best leaders are the ones who know how to weave a business philosophy in a way that gets communicated effectively to large bodies of people. And to that end, we have found that the STAR process and its attendant outputs provide an excellent way to communicate the organization's strategic journey and how the key initiatives and the people working on those initiatives are connected to it.

Strategy to Execution

With a clearly defined strategic plan, backed by a strong business philosophy and a well-orchestrated communications plan, we're now ready to put an execution process in place. In the next chapter, we present a tried-and-true approach we've helped leading companies implement. The ability to develop an integrated strategy-to-execution process is the critical step in delivering a ruthlessly executing company.

3

Portfolio Management Discipline

We are what we repeatedly do. Excellence, then, is not an act, but a habit.

—Aristotle

As noted in Chapter 2, "Strategic Recalibration and the Business Philosophy," the strategic recalibration process should be as important to a business as manufacturing a product and delivering it to customers, or any other critical process that is core to what a company does.

By establishing the strategy process as a key fundamental for your business, the table has been set for the execution process to meet your strategic goals.

Working with large global enterprises, we've found that the development of a portfolio management discipline is a critical element of any recalibration effort. Much as financial experts use portfolio management theory to manage financial investments, executives can manage their own strategic investments to maximize the likelihood of strategic success.

In this chapter, we examine how a portfolio management discipline can take your strategic plans from conception to execution and maximize success.

Portfolio Management Discipline

The performance portfolio framework that will be set out in these pages is a proven and valuable approach to executing against the strategic recalibration process outlined in the prior chapter. It can help business leaders prioritize the different investment opportunities and better focus their organizations. We first introduced this framework to our clients in the mid-1990s and subsequently in the book *Net Ready* as a way to assess IT investments. However, this framework is a valid mechanism with which to gauge any capital or resource-intensive investment—for example, a new plant, product, or acquisition. In fact, over the past decade, we've focused our efforts in helping our clients implement a single strategy-to-portfolio management process for their companies.

> ## Portfolio. What Portfolio?
>
> Every business has a portfolio of initiatives that make up its "spend." The problem is most leaders don't realize they have a portfolio, and, worse, they don't do a good job of managing it.

The purpose of the framework is to enable a fact-based rationalization or prioritization of investments and resources that are being allocated across a company. The framework suggests, for example, that a company might need to find a better balance between performance and growth activities in order to meet the goals outlined in its strategy-recalibration process. The overarching goal of the portfolio framework is to ensure that the efforts to which a company commits significant capital and human resources will provide the greatest return on strategy (ROS). To be clear, this may not equate to the highest return on investment (ROI). In some cases the right investment has a zero or negative ROI, but it will set the foundation for a longer-term goal of the company's.

For example, we've reviewed hundreds of enterprise technology investments, and in certain cases the initial investment in the company's core information system has had a poor ROI. However, the investment still made sense because it represented a critical building block in the company's overall business strategy. In one case, the investment was necessary to meet regulatory requirements, which were very hard to quantify for senior leadership.

The framework, therefore, is a useful device to help establish priorities, because, quite frankly, today's executives confront a multitude of opportunities and a plethora of decisions that can easily overburden them. Rather than set priorities, most simply take on too many unfocused activities.

Using the Performance Portfolio Framework

So how does one use the performance portfolio framework? We often employ this framework with clients in mapping exercises that help them understand the investments and projects currently underway and whether they are aligned with the strategic battlefields they must win. In addition, it helps leaders determine which business initiatives they should undertake and what their risk profiles should be. The mapping takes place around core drivers that shape the value of a company. The core drivers become the parameters within the portfolio framework for the mapping exercise. The framework allows a move away from the traditional performance/growth paradigm, thus unlocking various options in the selection of business initiatives.

Newness/innovation and business criticality are the two key variables that make up the axes of the framework and that drive the value of a company. These dimensions, selected from empirical evidence, are critical in predicting a company's value.

The first driver, newness/innovation, goes on the horizontal axis. Essentially, this defines what new value you will bring to the marketplace and, therefore, how much new value it will bring to your company. The question to be answered is, how new or innovative is the particular initiative? As you move along the horizontal axis from left to right, the left side of the chart is not so new, whereas the right side is extremely new. Moving from right to left, the more standard or established an initiative becomes, the less new or innovative it is.

The second driver, business criticality, goes on the vertical axis, with business initiatives in the bottom half representing less "business-critical" initiatives than those in the upper half. **Business criticality** essentially defines how vital an initiative is to your business strategies. It measures the degree to which a particular business initiative directly drives the core differentiating factors for your company. The more "business critical" something is, the more strategic it is to a company; therefore, it is more of a risk to a company if it's not executed effectively.

Mapping business initiatives along the two dimensions of innovation/newness and business criticality allows you to understand the impact of high-ranking initiatives on your organization.

Figure 3-1 shows the performance portfolio framework. You can use the framework to map the location of any business initiative and thus gain a better understanding of why you are doing a certain business activity at a certain time and stage.

The portfolio framework is organized into four quadrants along the two dimensions of business criticality and innovation/newness:

- **Run the Business**—The most basic, low-risk, noncritical operations of a business are placed in the bottom-left side of the framework. Run the Business initiatives are productivity driven and aim at cutting costs; they are not strategic or core differentiators to the company. They typically do not directly impact shareholder value. Not excelling at Run the Business efforts might place a company at risk, but doing them very well will not guarantee success. Understanding which of the Run the Business initiatives are really important and which you should stop doing is essential. The average company has too many investments in this area that are not essential.

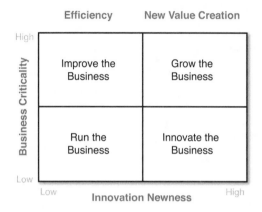

Figure 3-1 The performance portfolio framework

- **Improve the Business**—Initiatives in this quadrant are high in business criticality, medium in risk, and focus on transforming mission-critical initiatives, as well as stabilizing and improving core revenue. Projects and investments in this area are fundamental for competitive differentiation. They are more strategic than innovative, and are very essential to delivering value. The objective is to execute these efforts as efficiently and with as little friction as possible. For manufacturers, an example of this type of initiative is managing an organization's supply chain. Companies with limited investment or poor execution in Improve the Business initiatives place themselves at significant risk.

- **Innovate the Business**—Initiatives that fall within this quadrant experiment with new business models and new go-to-market strategies, and are low to medium in risk. The best advice with such initiatives is, if they work, keep them; if they don't—and most don't—shift your resources quickly.

By trying to create new markets and revenue growth in non-mission-critical areas, these initiatives tend to be new or innovative to the market, and if they fail, the business still survives. Not yet core to a business, they aim typically at new value creation as opposed to driving efficiency; they tend to focus on new organizational practices surrounding new products or services that might become strategic. The focus is on seeding new growth and new revenue streams. Choosing a select few that are focused is good; fishing for growth is not.

- **Grow the Business**—There are two types of Grow the Business initiatives: One comes from the top-left quadrant and helps drive topline growth of the core revenue base, whereas the other is born from Innovate the Business initiatives and creates change in the marketplace. This upper-right quadrant is the path-breaking, high-risk arena of business initiatives that involves transforming a core strategy or basic business approach. It can also involve transforming the nature of an entire market.

  High in business criticality, plus high in innovation, these business initiatives, when successful, can rupture an industry, altering the competitive balance among companies. Although relatively new, these initiatives quickly become strategic.

  These groundbreaking initiatives tend to be oriented toward new business models, new revenue streams, and innovative go-to-market strategies that have a very significant impact on the market itself. They are, by their nature, rare and fleeting (quickly turning into industry standards). What investments are you seeding for such opportunities? Seeding a select number of such opportunities is critical for future performance.

The Art and Science of Portfolio Management

In studying successful leaders, it became apparent that certain key rules are critical practices for effective portfolio management:

- **Rule 1: To drive business success, executives must move away from the ad hoc allocation of resources and toward a strategy of actively developing initiatives in each of the four quadrants of the portfolio framework.**

  Background: We've found that most companies, especially larger ones, have hundreds of projects underway, most of which do not drive value and are not aligned with the overall strategy. Without a clear-cut, highly defined strategy and key battlefields, the business leader finds that vast amounts of resources and precious blocks of time are easily wasted. By employing the portfolio framework, a business executive can make intelligent decisions that provide for a more reasoned, strategic, and efficient allocation of time, energy, and resources.

- **Rule 2: It is critical that business leaders build discipline into the portfolio-management process.**

  Background: As indicated earlier, most companies do not have an established process for managing the initiatives that fall across the company. Leaders who ruthlessly execute have in place a process by which they can

  - Intelligently compare initiatives across a set of strategic imperatives.
  - Prioritize initiatives across the organization on an informed basis.
  - Effectively allocate resources to drive successful execution.

- Better understand the ongoing costs and progress of the efforts.

- Gain better visibility into the value (financial and strategic impact) that investments deliver for the company.

- **Rule 3: Business leaders must earn the right to move from a lower to a higher state of both business criticality and innovation/newness**. There is a right of passage that allows one to migrate from quadrant to quadrant.

  Background: Earning the right to make this passage requires superior performance in Run the Business and Improve the Business projects. Too many right-side initiatives and investments without superior performance at the core is a recipe for trouble.

- **Rule 4: Business leaders need to focus on a select set of critical initiatives. The strategy of letting a thousand flowers bloom simply does not work**. Leaders who ruthlessly execute focus on a few critical initiatives that improve the core business and seed growth.

  Background: Although business leaders need to build a portfolio of initiatives with activity in each quadrant, *they will improve long-term performance only by succeeding in the activities in the upper quadrants.* The temptation to seed numerous growth opportunities is always strong, but successful leaders place their efforts on a select few (two or three at most). The urge to over-seed is especially powerful for companies whose cash flows and cash positions are strong because they feel they have the funds to experiment.

> ### Stop the Madness
>
> To reduce cost inefficiencies and to focus on strategic projects, one retail company implemented a company-wide process and tool to assess the expected revenue contribution of its projects and identify promising growth areas as well as areas of consolidation. This effort resulted in a 60 percent reduction in the number of active projects, while improving the financial and strategic impact.

- **Rule 5: Business leaders develop their own return on strategy (ROS) scoring system. Most companies prioritize projects based on a risk-adjusted return on investment (ROI) measure.** However, ROI is an incomplete and potentially misleading yardstick. Each quadrant instead should have distinct ROS characteristics that form the basis for the type of project portfolio a business executive builds. Accepting this measure focuses the organization on alignment between the strategic goals and the project portfolio it will execute.

  Background: Employing a financial portfolio as a metaphor for the portfolio of business initiatives is appropriate because most people are intimately familiar with the notion of financial portfolios.

  The four quadrants of the portfolio framework can be thought of as being analogous to investing in bonds (Run the Business strategies), blue-chip stocks (Improve the Business strategies), an IPO market or venture financing (Innovate the Business strategies), and emerging markets (Grow the Business strategies).

  To delve further into the metaphor:

  - **Run the Business** = bonds; low risk. Although you won't beat a market quickly, it's the smart, safe way to proceed.

- **Improve the Business** = blue-chip stocks; higher risk. These offer nice, steady returns. They are important in good and bad times.

- **Innovate the Business** = IPO market or venture financing; even higher risk. Many efforts fizzle out, but occasionally you hit pay dirt.

- **Grow the Business** = emerging markets; highest degree of risk. These strategies also offer the highest rewards.

This financial metaphor helps you realize that not all business initiatives are equal. In the same way that you would not expect the same returns from bonds as from high-tech stocks, you would not expect the same returns from Run the Business investments as those from Innovate the Business strategies.

Your selection of a financial portfolio is defined by your personal goals. For retired individuals, your goal may be preservation of capital with a dependable dividend stream. For young invincibles, it may be long-term growth to save for a home. The definition of what portfolio you pick (bonds, stocks, and so on) is heavily dependent on your strategy. Similarly for a business, once you've defined your strategic goals, developing a return on strategy measure that fits your business will ensure you're properly aligned in the investment decisions you make.

Figure 3-2 shows the performance portfolio framework viewed from the frame of reference of the financial metaphor.

- **Rule 6: Businesses that are underperforming versus their peers must focus more of their attention on Run the Business and Improve the Business initiatives.**

Background: Executives can get easily lured into a "let it ride" mentality that quickly brings them over to the Innovate the

Business quadrant. Such executives would be better off focusing on left-side initiatives. This is easier said than done. We have yet to know of an executive who is not tempted by, if not lured toward, high growth and quick profits.

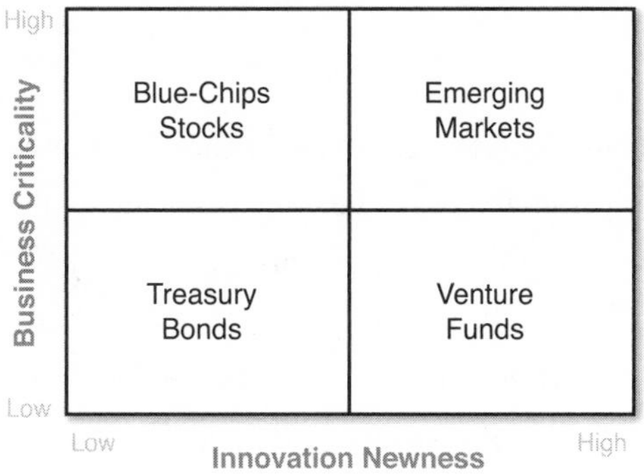

Figure 3-2   The performance portfolio framework using the financial metaphor

Yet, that misplaced focus—lurching to the right—leads executives to hold unhealthy business portfolios, thus incurring the wrath of the financial markets. When viewing a company's core business in decline, characterized by a swift drop in earnings, the markets do not look positively at growth-oriented investments and soon the company gets into financial trouble. Forced to tighten capital spending, it begins its cutbacks by killing off the very same tempting quick-growth initiatives.

Companies must learn to allocate their "spend"—their capital investments (and resources)—differently. Keep in mind that "best of breed" firms tend to allocate the vast majority of their spend on left-side initiatives—some 40 percent of their spend tends to be allocated to Improve the Business initiatives and 10 percent goes to right-side investments.

Is There a Doctor in the House?

In contrast to these leading companies, most companies have unhealthy portfolios. Our research indicates that more than 40 percent of companies allocate 80 percent of their capital investment and resources to Run the Business initiatives.

Most successful business leaders tend to recalibrate by focusing on Improve the Business projects. However, cost cutting alone is not enough; seeding future growth is an imperative as well. Still, right-side growth programs will fail without a strong operational base. Critical weaknesses in the core business must be addressed before a company can start allocating significant spending on growth efforts.

The goal of portfolio management is to ensure that the investments you choose are maximizing the return on your business strategy. But most companies do not achieve such a balance, leaving them with unhealthy portfolios. Most companies allocate attention to too many activities at once.

These companies are at significant risk. Not only do financial markets punish them as their earnings decline, but the same markets also scorn their growth initiatives, reflecting the failure of the companies to earn the right to grow. Other companies err by devoting most of their attention to growth and new value-creation activities (Grow and Innovate the Business quadrants).

What does a well-balanced portfolio look like? Or, to put it somewhat differently, what is the ideal outcome of portfolio management? Achieving a good balance does not at all mean having the same number of initiatives in each quadrant. The poor success rate of Innovate the Business and its fleetingness (lasting six to nine months) usually means that companies need a greater number of investment seeds than one would think. *The key is to focus on a few and then provide the needed funding and resources to foster success.*

Too often, businesses fall into "portfolio traps," which do not allow them to effectively align their investments with the results of their strategic recalibration. Among such traps are the following:

- **Hesitation**—For most companies that find themselves in tough environments, where business trends are emerging but not necessarily posing an immediate threat, it is natural to just wait and see. Added to this, there is often a lack of fact-based insight that makes visibility to these trends problematic.

- **Sticking with the familiar**—This portfolio trap is characterized by the Run the Business quadrant, where a company allocates more than 80 percent of its attention to these efforts. This trap is often hard to get out of even when there are compelling arguments and environmental signals to make changes.

- **Half-heartedness**—Some companies place many small bets on new initiatives, but end up very cautious. Without clear-cut revenue or profit prospects, it becomes difficult to justify large investments. Under pressure to bring in positive quarterly results, companies have trouble making long-term commitments. Although leaders face difficult tradeoffs between creating short- and long-term value, spreading investment resources across too many efforts ultimately dilutes the productivity of the portfolio.

- **Pioneering**—These companies are able to create radical, new products and transform an industry. Although it is tempting to be a bold innovator, the business leaders we studied avoided the "pioneering trap" by returning to basics, earning them the right to grow. Focusing excessively on breakthrough strategies probably means a company is not a leader.

A significant part of portfolio management is not optimizing the portfolio on ROI, which really is about one investment at a time, but on ROS—return on strategy. This means asking to what degree the investments you're making support your strategies, and what the return on those investments is in aggregate? Not all growth is good. Executives should not simply invest in the highest profit-returning projects, but rather they should *make sure that the kind of growth that is pursued creates value for the company.*

Among the critical qualities we found in the leaders we studied was an analytical, fact-based bent. The executives tended also to be unemotional about the act of strategic recalibration. For business leaders today, all too familiar with the increased rates of change in their industries, there is nothing more important than to analyze precisely what creates a return on strategy for their companies.

Defining an ROS metric for your company truly depends on the nature of your individual business. Your leadership team will need to decide how to weigh the principles discussed in this book—how to run, improve, innovate, and grow the business—against your company's strategic plan. For those companies whose strategy is focused on reinventing the core products, for example, improving measures for return on strategy may be more heavily weighted.

For those looking at innovating through the cloud, innovation metrics may be more heavily weighted in their ROS calculation. The purpose of creating an ROS measure is to both deepen and sharpen your prioritization of capital opportunities. It is the unfortunate truth that many companies do not embrace the kind of rigorous analytical process that is needed at such critical times, preferring to make decisions in an ad hoc fashion that keeps them from making true progress.

As part of that rigorous analysis, leaders must constantly supervise the initiatives that could help them create breakaway performance. They must treat each initiative as if it were a separate business, having the time and patience to uncover which initiatives are worth retaining and nurturing and which need to be killed.

Engaging in that same meticulous probing, executives must make sure that new initiatives fall within core parts of their businesses. This means pursuing operational excellence—in short, making certain they have the fundamentals of their businesses down. They must also make sure they do not neglect the growth side of their businesses, even in tough, challenging times.

Business leaders who pay attention to both the performance and the growth parts of their businesses simultaneously are truly engaged in portfolio management.

Maximizing Return on Strategy

To summarize, the way to maximize shareholder value is not to simply identify the greatest short-term profit-generating projects and execute against them. The result of such an approach is often that the company's resources become spread too thin, working against each other like a ball of string being pulled in too many directions.

We believe the key leadership elements to ruthlessly execute are as follows:

- Focus the company by investing the requisite time and effort to strategically recalibrate the company each year and set the business philosophy to remove cultural barriers.
- Create a portfolio of initiatives that maximize the return on your strategy.
- Ensure that the right processes are put in place to assess the progress of these initiatives, which should be reviewed on a quarterly basis.
- Actively measure the results of your investments to communicate the progress of your strategy and incentivize the team to meet the goals of your projects.

4

Cardinal Health Thrives on Culture of Reinvention

Taming Turbulence

Guiding a company through turbulent economic times takes tough leaders, but also creative ones. Having a healthy appetite for change also helps. For Cardinal Health—the $101-billion-a-year healthcare services company based in Dublin, Ohio—resilient and creative leadership has repeatedly revitalized the company as it navigated the twists and turns of the volatile healthcare industry.

Cardinal Health's executives call it "constant reinvention," and they will tell you that the very nature of their business demands it. Starting as a regional food delivery company more than 40 years ago, Cardinal Health has reinvented itself many times over, and in the process has turned into a vastly more valuable enterprise that today plays an essential role in the healthcare industry.

It has been a wild ride for a company that is now Ohio's largest and most profitable corporation, employing more than 34,000 people worldwide. These days, Cardinal Health hovers around number 20 on the Fortune 500 rankings, alongside names such as IBM and JPMorgan Chase. Within the pharmaceutical distribution industry, Cardinal vies for leadership with McKesson Corp. and AmerisourceBergen.

Cardinal Health has run into its share of rough patches, including setbacks that shook its stock price and investments that fell short of expectations. But the healthcare supply chain leader never fails to weather the storm and bounce back seemingly stronger than before, ready to drive a new round of growth. The secret to Cardinal Health's success rests in part on its unique culture of reinvention. And it has filled its ranks with executives who thrive in that culture and have expertise in areas that are so critical to prospering in today's evolving healthcare system.

One of those executives is Patty Morrison, Cardinal Health's executive vice president and chief information officer. Previously, Morrison served as CIO for Motorola, and before that as Office Depot's CIO. She has held senior positions at companies including General Electric, PepsiCo, Procter & Gamble, and Quaker Oats Co.

For Cardinal Health, navigating through the turbulence calls for a blend of leadership skills—a combination of steadfast commitment to Cardinal's core business values and an unusual tolerance for change. At its core, Cardinal Health is all about great execution and delivering value to customers. "We are a very operationally focused company," Morrison says. "We are great at day-in, day-out execution, doing the right things for our company, and doing the right things for our customers."

But the rote repetition of traditional business formulas only gets you so far. In fact, sticking only to the familiar models that worked for you in the past is a really bad idea, Cardinal executives will tell you, especially in a volatile sector such as healthcare where business disruptions are practically business as usual. As a result, the company needs to constantly pivot to address emerging opportunities for value creation. The lesson Cardinal Health teaches is that the capacity for constant transformation has to be in your organization's DNA. You have to do it all the time to ensure success over the long term.

In the case of Cardinal Health, much of that transformation is enabled by information technology. This makes the role of IT and the

CIO much more strategic, but also requires senior business leaders to develop an understanding for how emerging information technologies can play a role in creating new value.

Cardinal Health is a study in reinvention and a prime example of correct decision making in the face of business challenges. For Cardinal Health, this has required ongoing commitment to operational excellence and value creation. Over the years, Cardinal Health has built a corporate culture and recruited and nurtured leaders who embody all those principles.

Constant Transformation

Cardinal Health was founded in 1971 by Robert D. Waller as a food wholesaler that trucked groceries to regional supermarkets. The company quickly saw a better future in drug distribution, and in 1979 acquired the Bailey Drug Company. Thus, Cardinal Foods became Cardinal Distribution—the company's first reinvention. In the early 1980s, the NASDAQ-listed company, seeing a strategic advantage in size, pursued a string of acquisitions and mergers that would rapidly grow Cardinal to national scale. Soon it was branching into medical supplies, with its landmark acquisition of Allegiance Hospital Supply in 1998. Everything from surgical gloves to crutches to IV bags were now included in the company's product catalog. Cardinal Health was systematically broadening its portfolio.

Throughout this high-growth period, however, Cardinal Health maintained strategic discipline and never deviated from its focus on delivering value to customers. That mission fueled another strategy: helping hospitals save money by offering standardized products that rival the quality of brands costing a lot more. In an industry famous for steeply rising prices, and now under pressure to drive prices in reverse, hospital systems are increasingly looking for high-quality but value-priced alternatives. New product introductions such as an orthopedic trauma solution in 2013, which Cardinal sells in partnership with Emerge Medical, exemplifies Cardinal's effort to reverse the trend.

Today, Cardinal Health touches all points along the care continuum through a broad line of products and services delivered across a global distribution network. The company's scope of operations spans hospitals, physician offices, more than 18,000 pharmacies, and a home healthcare division serving more than a million patients with 30,000 products, laboratories, surgery centers, imaging centers, and medical clinics.

Few opportunities are off limits for Cardinal Health. Recently it moved into information-based services with an offering that helps customers track products through their supply chains. The service is taking off in places such as China, where it is strengthening the company's foothold in distribution-based services. In North America, Cardinal is poised to capture an increasing share of the burgeoning homecare market with its 2013 acquisition of AssuraMed, a national leader in the home delivery of medical supplies.

Shock Absorption

Keying into the necessity of constant transformation, Cardinal Health's leaders have put strategies in place for absorbing the inevitable shocks when they hit. Adopting a portfolio view of investments, for example, has helped them weather market fluctuations and stay focused on long-term profitability. "You have to constantly rebalance your portfolio," Cardinal's CIO Morrison says. "That requires an ongoing process of strategy work and targeted investments and development." A strong balance sheet—the product of Cardinal's meticulous focus on operational excellence—also helps the company bounce back from missteps.

And although not every move pans out, the experience of trying new things invariably pays dividends. Cardinal's decision to enter the business of medical equipment manufacturing is one example. In 1996, Cardinal acquired Pyxis, the maker of automated pill dispensers, and in 2004 bought Alaris, which makes medical infusion pumps. Both moves promised generous margins but began tying up more capital than executives were comfortable with (in effect draining funds away from core services lines). Then came the unexpected recall of one of its Alaris infusion pump models, a costly diversion at the time.

Rather than dwell on the setbacks, Cardinal recalibrated: In 2007, it spun off its clinical medical products division (CareFusion) that housed Pyxis and Alaris in a move executives described as "strengthening the core." Today, CareFusion is a fast-growing public company with revenues of more than $4 billion.

Although shedding certain ventures makes sense, so does "hanging in there" on others. Often this is about giving new business lines the time to evolve or allowing markets to mature. This discriminating approach reflects Cardinal's attention to operational excellence informed by rigorous financial control. Cardinal is superb at pivoting, and its discipline means that the company remains firmly grounded during the transition.

Peripheral Vision

Executing reinventions takes a special breed of leader, so Cardinal has invested heavily in developing leaders and talent in crucial areas. Establishing goals and metrics for leaders helps in this development, as does constant evangelizing. More important is finding the types of personality that match the needs of the business at any given point in its history. Startups, for instance, need leaders who can handle the uncertainty and intense promotion that go along with a young enterprise.

For the leaders of Cardinal Health, strategic thinking may be the best all-purpose skill to have, embodying critical capabilities such as paying attention to the market and anticipating the next big thing. Cardinal Health CEO George Barrett calls it "peripheral vision," and it's a valuable aptitude in an industry such as healthcare services where market disruptions can come out of nowhere. To succeed, you need to be able to perceive industry shifts three to five years before they hit and not get blindsided. The battlefields of today may not be the battlefields just a few years out.

Another essential skill: the ability to break through the walls that divide lines of business, such as rigid distinctions between different product "silos." It's easy to get lost in that inside-out view, Cardinal executives say, which tends to blind you to the bigger ideas that move markets. At Cardinal, executives call it having an "enterprise perspective," and it helps them foresee dramatic shifts.

It takes significant effort to step outside your operational box and become attuned to what's going on in the broader world—but that's what Cardinal Health executives have been forced to do time and time again. Paradoxically, this may require action-oriented executives to put aside their insistence on immediate, tangible results in favor of open-ended explorations of ideas that take time to incubate.

Another useful leadership trait is the ability to corral and harness diverse perspectives—which is why Cardinal Health executives frequently take to the field. They are constantly meeting with customers, suppliers, and policymakers in Washington. That same passion for fresh ideas spurs Cardinal executives to reach out to their counterparts in different industries. You'll frequently see them talking to non-healthcare distributors such as Sysco Foods and W.W. Grainger to gather insights.

The quest also takes the form of investments in new technologies that give executives a chance to soak up new thinking. Finally, Cardinal leaders say that simply traveling with colleagues on business trips can have the beneficial side effect of stimulating big-picture ideas. "It's a great tool," one executive said after joining Cardinal leaders on a trip to see the company's growing operations in China. "It just forces your team to get out of their internal-facing tactical discussions."

Cardinal Health's continuous transformation continues apace. Events took a sharp turn in 2013, when Cardinal and drug store giant Walgreens parted ways, putting a significant portion of Cardinal's revenue stream at risk (though a less significant share of its profit). But thanks to its culture of reinvention—of constant transformation— Cardinal was prepared for this latest twist. It had seen it before. "We have a game plan," as CEO George Barrett told the *Columbus Dispatch*. "We'll carry on."[1] In Cardinal Health's annual report Barrett wrote, "When it became clear we would not renew our contract with Walgreens we prepared to make the appropriate organizational and strategic adjustments." This was a year, the CEO concludes, "that had more than its share of twists and turns and from which we emerge stronger and more confident in our future."[2]

Endnotes

1. Wartenberg, S. (2013, March 20). Cardinal Heath faces uncertainty after losing Walgreen contract. *The Columbus Dispatch*. Retrieved from http://www.dispatch.com (full URL: http://www.dispatch.com/content/stories/local/2013/03/20/cardinal-health-loses-big-contract.html)

2. Cardinal Health, 2013 Annual Report, Dec. 31, 2012, p. 3, from Cardinal Health investor relations website, http://ir.cardinalhealth.com/files/doc_financials/annual/2013/2013_Annual_Report.pdf, accessed June 19, 2014.

Part III
Critical Capabilities

5

Recalibrating to Compete in Today's Market

Ruthless Execution Checklist

- Do you have a cost and working capital management program that is driven throughout the business?
- Is cloud-enabling your business a focused part of your leadership and execution agenda?
- Is customer success part of your DNA and integrated into key business units and functional areas?
- Do you effectively and swiftly manage out nonperformers?

It has been asserted throughout this book that if executives are to overcome current business setbacks, and minimize future setbacks, they must demonstrate an ability to consistently execute in the following three strategies:

- Leadership
- Critical capabilities
- Governance

This chapter looks at the second element that executives need to overcome business reversals: critical capabilities, which are the specific actions executives drive to break through performance walls.

Capabilities Are Not Competencies

Very much at the core (or heart) of what a company does, competencies are how the company differentiates itself. For a company such as Cisco Systems, a competency can be its sales force or its acquisition and integration capabilities; for a company such as GE, it might be its uncanny ability to create synergies among its businesses.

Critical capabilities, on the other hand, are the recalibrating actions that need to become part of the corporate fabric. They are the essential triggers or springboards required for improved performance.

The same point made in the earlier chapters on leadership holds true for critical capabilities: Leaders who have successfully broken through performance walls all have certain critical capabilities in common that are very visible.

In our last book, the companies we studied focused on several capabilities in their effort to strategically recalibrate: These included vigilant productivity management, strategic corporate transactions (mergers, acquisitions, and divestitures), and a passion for talent management.

These critical capabilities are still part of the business leader's arsenal today. The best companies maintain an unwavering focus on productivity management, which requires a close understanding of what makes their business models tick. Cutting to the bone or slashing costs across the board at a set percentage almost never works. Rather, leaders need to connect cost drivers to how their individual businesses create value and draw in customers, and then establish cost-management strategies to match.

We also believe that focused corporate transactions will continue to be a critical capability for companies in the current economy, which remains turbulent and uncertain. Consistently evaluating strategic acquisitions and divestitures of business and assets, both in good times and bad, is the hallmark of revitalization.

Finally, the leaders we have spoken to continue to be committed to talent management. Fundamentally that means putting the right people in the right places, and keeping them over the long haul. Part of this critical capability is the awareness of keeping only the best performers, getting rid of the bottom 10 percent of people who are not performing up to standard, and going through this weeding-out process on a regular basis (yearly) and thus upgrading the talent and performance pool.

Although these aptitudes are not going away as major differentiators for businesses in the years ahead, we are now seeing two new critical capabilities moving to the forefront of the leadership agenda:

- The "cloudification" of business
- Customer success management

Cloudification of Business

En route to San Francisco, a commercial airliner is showing what could be signs of trouble. Special sensors embedded in the inner workings of one of the jet engines detect a vibration pattern that indicates the onset of mechanical failure. Fortunately these "smart engines" have a voice of their own. Within seconds the machines are transmitting alerts to the pilot and ground crews, who mobilize to troubleshoot the performance issues even as the aircraft continues to fly. Before the plane touches down, maintenance teams have already assembled the parts they need to fix the engine and can predict how long the repairs will take. That, in turn, gives the airline enough lead time to reshuffle flights so that travelers avoid delays and missed connections.

A third wave of Internet innovation—epitomized by this aviation example—is fundamentally altering the way industrial machines and humans work together. The result is an emerging phenomenon we're calling the "cloudification" of business, which brings together intelligent, interconnected machines with the power of Big Data analytics and modern user experiences. Today, the cloudification of industrial companies is helping utility companies improve gas turbine performance, allowing hospitals to simultaneously enhance patient outcomes and throughput, and enabling railroads to maximize velocity on their rail networks.

In other sectors, from auto manufacturing to coffee retailers, firms are developing prototypes of "smart" products and services—and investing in entirely new business models—that run in the cloud. By merging data streams from sensors and other sources—and combining them with powerful analytics and simple-but-powerful user interfaces—airlines are creating proactive maintenance capabilities, shifting from a "can create" to a "fix-before-break" model. This transition may well transform the travel experience for passengers and permanently alter the economics of the aviation industry.

Another example is the coffee leader Starbucks. Its chief executive, Howard Schultz, recently announced that he has expanded his role in product innovation and digital retailing to adjust to technology-driven shifts in retail. Mr. Schultz plans to work closely with Starbuck's chief digital officer Adam Brotman and chief strategy officer Matt Ryan on their "next generation (of) retailing and payments initiatives," moving the company further into cloud-enabled services for its customers.[1]

These are just a few examples of what's now becoming possible in the new age of cloud-enabled businesses, an offshoot of the Web that is rapidly developing as a significant value-producing business platform across key sectors of the modern economy.

Increasingly businesses are looking for innovative ways to reinvent their products and services through ubiquitous sensors that gather and transmit data such as product quality, performance, and maintenance data as well as customer information such as environmental, social, and economic profiles to better serve these same customers in the future. These sensors are integrated with cloud-based networks that can marshal Big Data analytical resources and plug in to software applications that help companies better tackle technical and business problems. Indeed, the cloudification of business stands out as one of the best examples of how, in the words of web pioneer Marc Andreessen, "software is eating the world."[2]

The companies we studied are leveraging cloud-based applications and capabilities to drive new value for their customers. Ironically, this movement is not being driven by the high-tech industry, although it's true that many visionary technology firms are advocates and enablers of the cloud-based innovation wave. Rather, we are seeing companies such as Rockwell and GE as well as other mainstays of old-line industries take a leadership position in shaping how the cloud will impact business. However, realizing the cloud's potential will depend on many factors coming together at the same time. Namely, it will require the building of safe and secure industry and cross-industry technology platforms, the further evolution of a diverse development eco-system, and continuing efforts to design a captivating user experience that rivals the ease of consumer web applications.

Customer Success Management

When we talk to business leaders today, we are struck by their overwhelming interest in understanding their customers. They want to know what motivates their behavior and how they can keep them happy. They want to know where to invest to drive desired outcomes such as greater customer intimacy and retention.

Of course, customer satisfaction has always been a goal for business, but today the landscape is different and new forces are putting the concept of customer success squarely on the radar screens in the C-suite (and soon boardrooms as well) across the globe. Thanks to the digital revolution, and now the ascent of social media, the power relationship between businesses and customers has altered significantly. Customers are smarter, shop globally, and wield vast networks of online friends and colleagues to weigh their options and spread news. In many industries, companies have to battle price concessions and commoditization pressures. Moreover, it is expensive to get new customers, and even costlier to regain a lost customer. Part of the challenge is ensuring customer success: With switching costs getting lower in part to renewal and utility pricing models, and more options available to customers, it is imperative that companies take the time to understand and communicate the value they are delivering to customers.

Perhaps no single performance indicator holds as much influence in business today as customer loyalty. Indeed, analyst Mikael Blaisdell asserts that customer retention rates approaching 95 percent can literally double the valuation of a company compared to an 80 percent rate.[3] It's no surprise then to find in a recent survey of CEOs that "getting closer to customers" was judged to be one of three prerequisites for success in the twenty-first century.[4]

In order to address these pressures, companies increasingly need to reexamine how they deal with customers and their customer practices across the organization. The top performing companies we studied are ensuring their customers are successful by trying to put the customer center stage across key aspects and processes of their organization, including sales and support, procurement, product development, and contracts.

They are continually challenging their existing business practices by asking the following questions:

- Are our customers truly benefiting from our products and services?
- Are we doing enough to ensure our customers are successful?

These questions are top of mind for business leaders these days, and they are driving the development of a new critical capability: a set of customer-centric practices that we call "Customer Success Management." Customer Success Management is about institutionalizing customer success and customer value into critical parts of your organization in order to increase customer loyalty and financial performance. Across the B2B sector especially, the choice is becoming clear: Either you actively manage your customer relationships as a strategic portfolio of assets or you effectively cede control over them and your company's future to chance—or the competition.

Customer acquisition is only the very first step in what must be a long-term, scientifically engineered, and professionally directed strategy. The emerging capability of Customer Success Management embraces a set of capabilities around customer portfolio development, retention, and expansion. The long-range vision of Customer Success Management includes an integration of technology, marketing, sales, services and support, training, and product development that helps deliver customer success. The ultimate strategic goal of this capability is sustainable corporate profitability and growth. The methods employed (listed next) aim to make your customers as profitable and productive as possible:

- Continuous listening to the voice of the customer
- Constant improvement of customer experience
- Moving from a focus on products to a focus on customer value and business outcomes
- Monitoring and demonstrating the actual value being realized by customers

At the end of the day, customers, not market segments, are who you do business with. And they are not interested in your products, or worse yet, the features of your products (even if they seem to be asking about them). They are interested in the value you can offer them. We try to highlight these capabilities later in this book by looking at business software giant Oracle, which is perhaps not the first company that comes to mind when you think about customer advocacy and success. However, in recent years this company has embarked on a journey to become a leader in customer centricity, listening to and quantifying for its customers the value its solutions and services create as an integral part of its corporate DNA. Already this shift in focus is yielding real benefits, giving the technology leader significant adaptive power in one of the fastest evolving marketplaces around.

Endnotes

1. Marks, G. (2014, Feb. 3). What is Starbucks brewing for mobile payments. *Forbes.* Retrieved from http://www.forbes.com (full URL: http://www.forbes.com/sites/quickerbettertech/2014/02/03/what-is-starbucks-brewing-for-mobile-payments/)

2. Andreessen, M. (2011, Aug. 20). Why software is eating the world. *The Wall Street Journal.* Retrieved from http://www.online.wsj.com (full URL: http://online.wsj.com/news/articles/SB10001424053111903480904576512250915629460?mg=reno64-wsj)

3. Blaisdell, M. (2012, June 15). No churn: Customer Success and the valuation of a SaaS company. *The HotLine Magazine Archive.* Retrieved from http://www.mblaisdell.com (full URL: http://mblaisdell.com/2012/06/15/no-churn-customer-success-and-the-valuation-of-a-saas-company/)

4. "Capitalizing on Complexity: Insights from the Global Chief Executive Officer Study." IBM Institute for Business Value. May 2010. http://www.ibm.com/ceostudy

6

Managing Customer Success: The Last Mile of Customer Loyalty

Ruthless Execution Checklist

- Do you measure the ROI/Business Impact of the top five solutions at your top five customers?
- Do you proactively and annually present the value of your solutions to your most valued customers?
- Do most of your customers look at you as a vendor or a strategic partner?
- On sales calls, are you meeting with tactical operators or key business leaders?

These days, conversations in executive suites and boardrooms increasingly turn to topics such as customer loyalty, retention, and churn. We're seeing more leaders deploying "listening posts" to gather feedback on what customers are thinking. Indeed, according to Aberdeen Group, some 70 percent of companies judged to be "best in class" in customer experience say they use customer feedback in a strategic way.[1] And in a recent survey, CEOs said that "getting closer to customers" was one of three prerequisites for success in the twenty-first century.[2]

This wasn't necessarily true just a decade ago. To be sure, catering to customer needs has always made for good PR and marketing, but the urgency around customer experience that we see today was absent. "Build it and they will come" made sense back then, and for good reason. In many industries, especially in industrial sectors, customers were stuck with incumbent suppliers, having sunk sizable costs into their proprietary systems. Switching to alternatives was painful and risky.

The evolution of IT infrastructure is a great example. In the infrastructure's infancy, customers were tied to expensive mainframe systems, then these solutions were replaced with commodity servers that were surprisingly powerful, cheaper to own, and easy to scale out. Today, these same companies are moving to even more cost-effective "virtualized" computing platforms. Here, incumbents in the commodity hardware business, such as Dell and Lenovo, are being challenged by cloud-based newcomers such as Amazon, Salesforce.com, and Rackspace.

Power Shift

Why are business heavyweights finally getting serious about customer success? The leaders we studied pointed to a host of factors, including technology-induced disruptions that have altered the ground rules of doing business. New forces are putting customer success—how to understand and manage it—right at the top of the corporate agenda.

These changes reflect the continuing impact of the digital revolution, augmented now by the ascent of social media, which abruptly shifted the balance of power between sellers and buyers in the marketplace. Bottom line: Customers have seized the upper hand, and it's directly influencing the strategies and investment priorities of businesses. Enablers of consumer power include online shopping

powerhouses Amazon and eBay, where consumers effortlessly compare products, and social networks such as Facebook and Yelp, where
users trade opinions and ignite demand. Consumer power puts pricing pressure on manufacturers and squeezes margins. Conversely, it
gives innovators an edge, especially those that understand what makes
buyers tick.

What worries executives now is the spread of these consumer-
like market forces to traditional business-to-business sectors, where
a wave of upstarts are challenging business models by allowing customers to rent software over the Internet instead of buying it. They
are overtaking markets once dominated by companies that sold and
installed software "on premises" at customers' computer centers.

Leading the way here are companies such as Salesforce.com
(founded by ex-Oracle executive Mark Benioff), which has become a
dominant force in the market for managing sales teams. Cloud-based
Workday is doing the same for managing corporate workforces. More
recently, rapidly growing Constant Contact, Marketo, and Eloqua
are transplanting the management of marketing and direct-mail cam-
paigns from office desktops into the cloud. Seeing the shift, incumbents such as Microsoft and Oracle are driving with their own cloud
offerings through R&D and acquisitions (such as Eloqua.)

In other words, we are seeing the ushering in of a subscription
economy. Not only in software, but other industries such as media,
publishing, entertainment, healthcare, and others.

Why Loyalty Matters

Although many cloud upstarts are eating the lunch of brick-and-
mortar businesses, they are also finding they need to work harder to
hang on to customers. That's because customers can easily switch
to another service or just not renew their subscription if they're not
realizing value from the product. In this environment of "trying and

buying," loyalty becomes clearly linked to the daily experience that your customers have with your products and services, and the actual business value they're seeing. The #1 reason customers leave is that they do not perceive an ROI from your solutions.

In reality, fostering customer loyalty is the best and cheapest way to grow your business. According to Bain & Company, it costs six to seven times more to attract a new customer than it does to keep an old one.[3] What's more, according to a study co-authored by Wharton professor Shawndra Hill, it's significantly more likely that you'll sell products and services to an existing customer than a brand-new one.[4]

This explains why customer loyalty has become one the most influential performance indicators in business today. In fact, analyst Mikael Blaisdell says that customer retention rates approaching 95 percent can double the valuation of a company compared to an 80 percent rate. Customer churn, he calculates, acts like a negative interest rate, compounding lost revenue year after year and ultimately putting the brakes on your business' growth potential.[5]

Moving Beyond Loyalty to Customer Success

Companies have made significant progress in managing and measuring customer loyalty, with great success. We now see more companies experimenting with new approaches to how they promote their achievements in customer loyalty and the value created from their products and services. They are funding reexaminations of their customer-facing practices, from how they sell and support products to whether customers have a say in developing new products. They are setting up systems to try to understand what their customers think and feel, what their daily experience is like, and what things could be changed to make that experience better.

Still there is a long way to go: McKinsey, for example, recently reported that only 12 percent of marketing spend goes toward customer retention, while more than half goes to acquiring new customers.[6] When it comes to sales practices, the facts are even worse, with the majority of sales efforts focused on new customer acquisition.

Our research shows that companies that are great at inspiring loyalty are also diligent about collecting customer experience data from all kinds of sources and analyzing it to uncover key correlations. Doing so can generate key strategic insights, such as how much sales are impacted by call center interactions, or how churn is affected by customer-friendly (or unfriendly) contracting practices. Putting together a clear picture of your customers' experience requires breaking down walls between lines of business so that information can flow freely to enable multidimensional analysis.

Three Kinds of Customer Loyalty (per Bob Hayes)

Most companies will benefit by looking at customer loyalty more broadly:

- **Advocacy loyalty** is about the customers loving you. This affection manifests itself as positive word-of-mouth/mouse behaviors.

- **Purchasing loyalty** is about customers expanding and deepening their relationship with you. They do this by buying new and different offerings from you.

- **Retention loyalty** is about customers not defecting to another company. Only about 12 percent of marketing spend goes toward customer retention.

Reference: Bob Hayes infographic with stats:
http://businessoverbroadway.com/two-more-customer-experience-facts-and-suggestions-you-cant-ignore-infographic

Harvesting Value—The Last Mile of Customer Loyalty

Your ability to sell in this new economy will in a larger part be connected to your ability to deliver measurable business outcomes to your existing customers. Are your customers truly benefiting from your products and services? Are you doing enough to ensure your customers are successful? These are questions that are top of mind for business leaders these days, and they are driving the development of a new critical capability—a set of customer-centric practices that we call "Customer Success Management."

We define customer success management as a disciplined way of making your customers' success and associated outcomes part of your corporate DNA. Marketing, sales, and service/support must have customer success central in their charter, as shown in Figure 6-1.

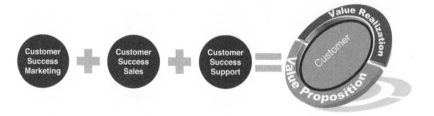

Figure 6-1   Customer Success Management

Customer acquisition is only the first step in what must be a long-term, scientifically engineered, and professionally directed strategy aimed at proactively managing customer success. The effort will involve integrating technology, marketing, sales, services and support, training, and product development in a coordinated way to make your customers as profitable and productive as possible.

In our study of companies that have made the transition to customer centricity, three strategies stand out:

- *Set up listening posts.* The best companies invest in programs that continuously monitor customer opinion, analyze feedback, and promote two-way collaborative relationships.

- *Sell business outcomes, not products or services.* Customers want solutions that solve real-life problems. News flash! Customers don't care about your products. They care about business outcomes you can help them achieve and how you can make them a hero. When you move beyond a transactional mindset of simply selling products to actually helping customers grow and innovate, you create the conditions for building a fiercely loyal customer base.

- *Ensure adoption.* Customer-centric companies know that the initial sale is only the beginning of a process. More important is making sure your customers are successfully implementing and using your solutions—and if not, why not.

The end goal is to help your customers realize maximum value from the products and services you sell—which by the way is a great way of guaranteeing customer loyalty and robust revenue streams. Nevertheless, surprisingly few organizations are seriously focused on helping customers harvest value from what they sell. Part of the problem is communication: Our research indicates that companies can reduce their customer churn to about 2-3 percent (from the average 10-20 percent) by proactively managing customer value and proving to the customer the value of their products and services.[7]

To capture solid returns, you must be able to persuasively demonstrate the business impact or ROI of your offering well before the sale—and then back that up after the sale by documenting exactly how the customer has harvested that value. It comes down to understanding, demonstrating, and communicating the actual value being realized by your customers. We see this as truly the "last mile of customer loyalty." The better you can do this, the more your prices will be seen as reasonable and the more you'll be perceived not just as a vendor but as a strategic business partner.

Our research found that companies employing effective customer management practices reduce churn and recapture millions of dollars in revenue per year in the process. Putting in place compensation programs based on profitability of accounts is a necessary step, but not enough. Beyond that you need to make value realization an integral part of your culture—part of your corporate DNA—and equip your teams with value-selling processes and value-based sales tools. Doing so will turn you into a partner that provides solutions that meet real needs and delivers on its promises.

As we indicated earlier, marketing, sales, and support must change. Many of the sales tools, conversations, and collateral that the sales teams use (and the marketing content companies produce) don't matter. Companies must transform the tools and skills of those interacting with customers to be centered on business outcomes that matter to their customers.

To help make customer success part of your agenda, we suggest the following steps:

1. Customer Success Marketing:
    - Develop content that customers care about and is focused on business outcomes
    - Align the content with the customer's and salesforce's buying and selling cycle
    - Distribute your content through a mix of channels (in-person, print, online, social, video, etc.) and measure its business impact
2. Customer Success Sales:
    - Engage with your customers to understand their businesses, what's at the top of their minds, and how they are measured

- Problem solve with your customer and then justify the business solution
- Help develop measureable business outcomes to gauge customer success

3. Customer Success Support

- Help your customers understand the value they are actually accomplishing
- Understand your customer's adoption challenges and help overcome these challenges to influence their success
- Guide your customer to achieve the full potential of their business solution

In Chapter 8, "Oracle's Journey to Customer Centricity," we attempt to highlight these capabilities by looking at business technology leader Oracle—perhaps not the first company that comes to mind when you think of outstanding customer service. But that was before the company set out to become customer centric and made listening to customers an integral part of its corporate DNA. Already the new focus is yielding benefits, giving the technology leader new adaptive power in one of the fastest evolving marketplaces around.

Endnotes

1. Original Aberdeen report (Aberdeen Group, Customer Experience Management: Engaging Loyal Customers to Evangelize Your Brand) no longer available online. Citation found at: Cox, K.J. (2014, March 6). Big data kills by a thousand cuts. Retrieved from Linkedin.com June 24, 2014. (full URL: https://www.linkedin.com/today/post/article/20140306054257-110384-big-data-kills-by-a-thousand-cuts)

2. "Capitalizing on Complexity: Insights from the Global Chief Executive Officer Study." IBM Institute for Business Value. May 2010. http://www.ibm.com/ceostudy

3. Cited in: Ho, V. (2013, March 14) Master the art of customer loyalty. Retrieved from Inc.com. (full URL: http://www.inc.com/victor-ho/master-the-art-of-customer-loyalty.html)

4. Cited in Knowledge@Wharton (https://knowledge.wharton.upenn.edu) Network-based Marketing: Using Existing Customers to Help Sell to New Ones (full URL: https://knowledge.wharton.upenn.edu/article/network-based-marketing-using-existing-customers-to-help-sell-to-new-ones/)

5. Blaisdell, M. (2012, June 15). No churn: Customer Success and the valuation of a SaaS company. *The HotLine Magazine Archive*. Retrieved from http://www.mblaisdell.com (full URL: http://mblaisdell.com/2012/06/15/no-churn-customer-success-and-the-valuation-of-a-saas-company/)

6. Cited here: http://www.shopparity.com/blog/4-customer-retention-if-only-rappers-had-this-equation-to-make-a-dollar-out-of-fifteen-cents; and also cited here: http://www.asklistenretain.com/important-customer-statistics/

7. "Measuring the ROI of Customer Success Management Solutions," Gainsight-Mainstay, 2014 – page 3. (URL: http://www.gainsight.com/sites/default/files/Mainstay-ROI-CSM-WP.pdf)

7

The Internet's Third Wave:
The Cloudification of Business

In the previous chapter we asserted that global business is poised to experience a surge of technology innovation that will alter the way machines and people work together. The trend is what we're calling the "cloudification of business," which brings together intelligent, interconnected machines with the power of Big Data analytics and compelling user experiences. However, realizing the cloud's full potential will require organizations to revisit how they interact with customers and drive changes across core parts of their organizations.

What is cloudification? We believe this will be the third wave of the Internet revolution in which products and services are being put on the cloud for customers to use as they need. The significance of such a trend is far reaching. First, it radically changes the investment equation for customers by lowering upfront capital requirements and reducing switching costs. Second, it has the potential to lower barriers to entry and switching costs across business-to-business markets. Incumbents such as Cisco in the networking world are making the change, but the transition is anything but trivial, as established business models and channel partnerships will be put at risk.

What does it mean to "cloudify" your business? Cloudification is about transforming/digitizing your products and services into an offering or platform that is accessible/usable on the Internet or cloud. We say platform, because in some cases, companies have the ability to open up their product as a platform for others to add value and new offerings to it. Cloudification typically spans three domains, as illustrated in Figure 7-1. Its foundation is made up of networks of intelligent machines, controllers, and other physical assets—such as smartphones, sensor-embedded jet engines, wearable sensors, location-aware locomotives, and smart wind turbines. The platform, in some cases, will be adopted across industries and include capabilities such as collecting enormous amounts of data. In fact, estimates are that by 2030 the digital universe will be 1,000 times the size of today's environment.[1] Companies will need to master Big Data advanced analytics that channel sensor-generated data streams and transform them into relevant business intelligence. Then there are the product and services teams—people at work who will tap these analytics to invent new product designs, create new service capabilities, and make timely decisions to optimize operations.

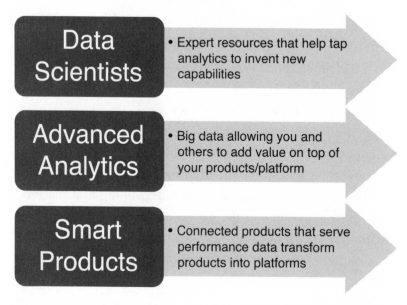

Figure 7-1   Cloudification core competencies: from smart products to big data analytics to data scientists

The business leaders we studied are expecting the cloud—like the two waves of Internet innovation before it—to seriously challenge traditional formulas for success. Here are a few examples of how very traditional and long-standing industries have changed:

- **Aviation**—Jet engines are able to talk to ground crews.
- **Healthcare**—Ambulance equipment is able to send patient data to the ER prior to arrival.
- **Oil and gas**—Well equipment sensors can talk to engineers miles away, alerting them of a part malfunction.
- **Retail**—Starbucks enters the banking industry with a mobile payment platform.
- **Technology**—Online retailer Amazon challenges the technology industry with its cloud-enabled infrastructure service.
- **Public safety**—Google Glass is used by patrol officers to record criminal activity during police intervention for use during trials.
- **Energy**—Wind turbines can talk to each other for maintenance optimization

These are not trivial developments. Indeed, we are predicting enormous economic impacts as more firms learn to monetize sensor data. By one estimate, the business cloud has the potential to add $19 trillion to global GDP by 2030.[2] These payoffs come from helping businesses reduce support costs, improve product design, cut energy consumption, improve health outcomes, extend the world's natural resource base, and more.

Why Now?

A confluence of trends helps to explain why it's now possible to fully commercialize sensor data and exploit its productivity and innovation potential. Here is what's driving the so-called "Internet of Everything":

- **Rapid technology innovation**—Breakthroughs in miniaturization, ruggedization, and processing power, coupled with a steady decline in sensor prices, has enabled engineers to embed more sensors in nearly every product. The result: surging numbers of machines connected to the Internet and a rise in the value of the network as a whole.

- **Economic and regulatory pressure**—Market challenges ranging from rising healthcare costs to increased governmental regulatory scrutiny (in 2012, 60 percent of U.S. companies retained outside counsel for regulatory investigation, up from 55 percent in 2011[3]) are forcing companies to find new ways to track and monitor products and services more closely.

- **Consumer behavior changes**—Generational familiarity with technology has reached mass consumer acceptance. With the advent of the smartphone and the mass commercialization of the Internet, with companies such as Amazon, Facebook, OpenTable, and so on, the business cloud has become a part of everyone's daily life. Companies must reset expectations of how they interact with their customers and anticipate new services and solutions to meet their technophilic expectations.

- **Social and demographic shifts**—Faced with an aging workforce (more than half of current workers are expected to retire in the in next five to eight years), companies have been scrambling to find new ways to manage their customers, products, and supporting infrastructure. Such demographic shifts work in favor of businesses with the foresight to embrace connected, content-rich Internet platforms.

Did You Know?

Today, more than 20 percent of Internet traffic originates from noncomputing devices. By 2020, some 50 billion machines will be plugged in to the Internet.[4]

The cloudification of the discrete manufacturing industry is a $2 trillion opportunity.[5]

By 2030, there will be an estimated 1 trillion sensors on the Earth—150 sensors for every human.[6]

Innovation Challenges

By no means is the rise of the business cloud a guaranteed game changer for every company. Significant work lies ahead for companies to transition to this new environment. Businesses must, in most cases, develop an ecosystem of innovators to work together to capture the most profitable opportunities. To start with, businesses must build competencies in key technology areas, such as harnessing data flows from intelligent machines and guarding against cyber threats. These competencies will form a portfolio of skills that enterprises will use to capitalize on opportunities. Seven areas of opportunity are discussed in this section.

Smart Products and Services

Machines deployed in industrial and consumer settings need to withstand extreme conditions. (Think of offshore oil wells, airplanes, Fitbit wearable sensors, and GoPro cameras.) Opportunities exist for companies able to design sensors that perform flawlessly in the harshest environments and that easily "plug and play" with the people or machines they monitor. Moreover, because communications will need to be instantaneous and failsafe, businesses will need to beef up their data network security to levels far exceeding what is commonly accepted for uses such as smartphones and online shopping. (When it comes to jet engines in flight, for instance, "downtime" is not an option; the same goes for consumers' healthcare information that's worn on their wrist.)

Structured and Unstructured Data Management

Knowing how to manage data flows from smart machines will become a big differentiator for companies investing in the business cloud, and new standards will need to be developed in this area. This will present big opportunities for innovators, especially as more smart machines are deployed. The ability for companies to collect a myriad of data formats—both structured and unstructured—will be critical to this effort. New cloud-based solutions providers such as Splunk will help businesses organize and manage this data. New data center technologies such as server and storage virtualization solutions (for example, UCS servers from Cisco and ConvergedSystem from HP) and integrated data appliances (for example, Exadata appliances from Oracle) will help companies flexibly and cost-effectively shift number-crunching duties to available computing resources.

Asset Management

Companies are looking at cloudification as a way to improve how they manage expensive assets such as gas turbines, locomotives, and hospital MRIs. Current asset management solutions are good at bookkeeping but they are incapable of "listening" to a machine's vital signs—which is exactly what the cloud can do. Expect more companies to start using sensor data, cloud connectivity, and Big Data analytics to detect and automatically remediate maintenance problems before they go critical.

Big Data Analytics

The truth is, most companies today are already drowning in data, but at the same time are starved for practical insights that can be used to optimize operations. In the age of the cloudification of businesses, Big Data analytics will play a leading role in taming the data torrent—not an easy task given the diversity of sources and types. The key to make Big Data analytics valuable to your business is the advent of highly complex statistical applications that comb through massive amounts of data to find patterns in seemingly unrelated environments coupled with data analysts who can apply these insights gleaned from one domain to solving challenges in another.

Designing Compelling User Experiences

For cloudification to take off, user experiences will need to become more compelling. For example, current industrial applications and interfaces that run factories are overloaded with irrelevant details and lack the lightning-fast response, easy navigation, mobility, and collaboration capabilities of consumer environments. Attracting top-notch application design talent will be crucial in this effort. We're already seeing early examples of this opportunity in the consumer space with smart home applications such as those from Nest, connecting your HVAC system with intelligent controls.

Security and Governance

Industrial and consumer firms alike are justifiably cautious about moving to the business cloud too quickly, with cyber security and reliability remaining top concerns. Innovators will tackle this challenge by engineering "industrial-grade" cloud infrastructures and military-grade cyber defenses that can thwart any security threat. Companies will need to adopt rigorous governance models to securely administer the federated roles and responsibilities within these environments.

Business leaders will also need to create a governance and operating model that addresses how value is shared from the industry data that is collected.

Business Model Transformation

Arguably the biggest challenge will be for established companies with established products and business models. What we are seeing in many industries, certainly led by high-tech, is the transition from products to services. In this service-centric world, traditional products are being integrated with technology-enabled services, where what matters most are the outcomes or results that the service can deliver. It is this transition to "business outcomes" that will challenge incumbents the most because it challenges the core of what the company does and how it makes money. In other words, customers are going to want to pay for the results of the service, or how much of that service they actually use, rather than the products that make up that service. Companies are so used to trying to win the feature game. They innovate by adding incremental new features and capabilities to their offering. The pricing model changes, partnership skills, service capabilities, and added financial risks that come from delivering a result versus a product may be too much for some to handle, whereas others will seize these opportunities.

Getting Ready for Cloudification

A business can take the following steps now to prepare for cloud-enabled innovation:

- Start by identifying opportunities that reinvent the way you connect with your customers. How can you transform your products or services into a platform that allows you and others to create added and differentiated value. How can you use sensors in your products to support the customers' use of your product? What are new services to enhance that experience?

- Then, within your organization, design new solutions and offerings that are cloud based. How can the integration of the cloud meet the new opportunities outlined in the previous section?

- Identify value-creating applications and drive a rapid iterative development process.

- Forge smart build/buy/partner strategies to seed business cloud initiatives.

- Begin building advanced data management capabilities and securing access to data analytics and scientific talent that dovetail with planned initiatives.

- Develop effective governance models that elevate the importance of managing Big Data and data platforms.

Technology firms will be the key to driving the innovations that lie ahead, helping invent, pilot, and refine the cloud. These solutions will feature technologies and protocols uniquely suited to cloud-based environments and applications—not just simple adaptations of the consumer Web. Now is the time for technology leaders to forge creative partnerships with traditional businesses to explore opportunities to tackle new ways to serve customers and unlock new value-creation opportunities.

Get ready for cultural shifts as the cloud gains traction. Earlier generations of workers with industrial hands-on machine-maintenance experience or consumer-based product management will give way to new ranks of data-driven technicians trained in predictive algorithms. Mission-critical "tribal" knowledge from earlier generations will need to be translated into the new interconnected, cloud-enabled, mobile environment.

What's in a Name?

Cloudification, Industrial Internet, Internet of Things, Internet of Everything, The Internet of the Customer—these are some of the latest buzzwords in technology and business circles. But what's the difference? The concepts are closely entwined and refer to the same basic idea of becoming closer to your customer through the cloud-based solutions that connect us to intelligent machines. Each term has its genesis from a specific focus for the author; for the Internet of Things, GE has a focus on building smart products for their customers. The Internet of Everything broadens the focus to all industries by network-enabling all industries, and the "cloudification of business" looks at the critical capabilities required to manage and succeed in this new wave of Internet solutions.

The Next Productivity Revolution

Just a 1 percent gain in fuel efficiency over 15 years would yield $30 billion in savings in aviation and $66 billion in the power-generation industry, whereas a 1 percent efficiency gain would yield $63 billion in the healthcare industry and $27 billion in the rail industry.

(Source: Peter Evans and Marco Annunziata, "Industrial Internet: Pushing the Boundaries of Minds and Machines," 2012)

One of the true pioneers in this area is likely a surprising case study. Rockwell International is a mainstay of the industrial industry—with its products in many of the largest and most successful factories across the globe. What's truly fascinating is that this old-world, traditional company has demonstrated the ability to lead its customers by cloudifying its products and services to enhance the value it provides to its customers.

Endnotes

1. "Big Data: The Next Frontier for Innovation, Competition and Productivity," McKinsey Global Institute Report

2. Peter Evans and Marco Annunziata, "Industrial Internet: Pushing the Boundaries of Minds and Machines," http://www.ge.com/docs/chapters/Industrial_Internet.pdf

3. Alanna Byrne, "Facts & Figures: Corporate counsel report increased litigation, regulatory investigations," Inside Counsel, 2013

4. http://www.cisco.com/web/about/ac79/docs/innov/IoT_IBSG_0411FINAL.pdf

5. Bryan Tantzen, "Manufacturing IOT POV Presentation," Cisco, 2013

6. "Intelligent Systems: the next big opportunity," IDC, 2011

8

Oracle's Journey to Customer Centricity

We will now turn to a great example of how a global information technology powerhouse, facing profound market shifts, reinvented how it relates to customers. The story of Oracle demonstrates the transformative power of *critical capabilities* to energize the company, and in doing so, build an atmosphere where *ruthless execution* became the highest value.

For more than three decades, the Oracle name has been synonymous with databases. Year after year, Oracle led the world in this category of software and continues to hold the top spot today. Founded by Larry Ellison, Bob Miner, and Ed Oates in the 1970s as Software Development Laboratories, the company adopted the name Oracle in 1982 to align itself more with its primary database product. In 1989, the fledgling company moved to the northern end of Silicon Valley and built its iconic headquarters—a cluster of glassy towers on the shores of San Francisco Bay.

The company endured its share of growing pains. In 1990, it reported its first-ever loss and shed hundreds of employees. But that was quickly erased by an Internet-propelled growth spurt in the 1990s and early 2000s. Oracle branded an Internet-inspired version of its database with the "i" suffix, and later introduced a "g" version to designate the next generation of "grid"-compatible products.

In 2004, after a high-profile battle, Oracle spent $10.3 billion to acquire PeopleSoft, one of the leading makers of software for managing human resources and other business applications. The acquisition represented a watershed event for Oracle, marking the start of a strategic recalibration as the database leader sought to become a more complete technology provider. For although it had built a strong market position in the database space, Oracle had yet to realize its larger vision of becoming the number-one provider of enterprise software—or business applications that run on top of databases to help companies manage everything from their financial books to their supply chains.

Oracle's new strategy was two-prong: It would push internal R&D efforts to enlarge the company's "solution footprint" and capture new markets, and it would acquire key capabilities and market share through strategic purchases. Oracle's buying spree lasted a decade. Following PeopleSoft, it went on to acquire Siebel Systems, the number-one provider of customer relationship management software, for $5.8 billion. Next came performance management software company Hyperion for $3.3 billion, followed by the acquisition of middleware company BEA Systems, for $7.3 billion. Oracle capped off the buying streak with the $7.4 billion takeover of Sun Microsystems. In between were purchases of scores of smaller, niche players in the IT sector that Oracle hoped would endow it with the technology and industry-specific capabilities it needed to grow.

Challenges

Early in the buying boom, however, Oracle ran into a challenge that was new to the company: how to convince customers arriving by acquisition that it was serious about defending their interests? Although Oracle had built its market dominance on the strength of an undeniably great database product, this very success also bred what more than a few observers perceived to be an aggressive—even arrogant—culture. How would this reputation mesh with customers accustomed to dealing with a more collaborative and people-centric company?

Even longtime Oracle customers admitted they were put off by the company's brashness. The attitude took a variety of forms but often came out during contract negotiations that many customers described as "adversarial" and "painful." Customers also complained of Oracle's narrow transactional focus that always came down to selling products—the more the better. Missing on the Oracle side was the ability to understand its customers' business needs or to help them brainstorm new strategies. Collaborative sessions with Oracle in which customers might influence the future development of the company's software—to the benefit of both parties—generally were absent.

The contentious PeopleSoft acquisition, it turned out, became a test case for Oracle's strategic recalibration—its embrace of a new way of relating to customers that would inform its remarkable journey to customer centricity, a process of that continues today. In some ways, the contrast between the two companies could not have been starker. Founded in 1987 by Ken Morris and Dave Duffield, PeopleSoft was a pioneer of the ERP market, and its customers were famously loyal. Consequently, many were unsettled by the prospect of being absorbed by a vendor such as Oracle with a history or turning a deaf ear to its own customers.

Undeterred, Oracle set out to change the way it related to customers. To prosper, executives knew the company had to forge new connections with customers and demonstrate a collaborative approach to working with them—a far cry from the adversarial posture it had assumed for so many years. Essentially, Oracle needed to develop a new critical capability to take the company forward.

In the fall of 2004—around the same time the PeopleSoft takeover was making headlines—Oracle executives began an investment to transform its customer relationships. Oracle veteran Jeb Dasteel, previously with the company's consulting organization, was tapped to spearhead the effort. "We had a fabulous reputation as a very strong engineering organization and a good, strong, aggressive sales organization," Dasteel explains. Yet Oracle lacked the critical capability that it needed to make PeopleSoft customers feel comfortable and sufficiently confident to stay put or even deepen their business connections with the database leader. Many harbored concerns that Oracle would fail to develop and improve on the "legacy" PeopleSoft line of products, potentially leaving businesses in a lurch down the road. Many worried that Oracle might cut off support and force a switch to lesser products.

Regardless, Oracle needed to move fast. In the wake of its multi-billion-dollar PeopleSoft deal, the company was coming under pressure to show investors evidence of financial discipline and progress toward reaping operational synergies. "All of that became our burning platform for customer retention," Dasteel said.

The Transformation

Oracle wasted no time getting started. The first order of business: calming the nerves of PeopleSoft customers who were worried that Oracle might abandon their favorite business applications and then steer them to Oracle's own products. The company's "Apps Unlimited" and related lifetime support programs, launched shortly after the acquisition, helped head off defections. Still, getting an organization the size of Oracle—at the time employing 50,000 people spread over dozens of countries—to fundamentally change its attitude toward customers would hardly be a trivial task.

Efficiencies dictated a global perspective, so Oracle formed a new organization—called Global Customer Programs—with the express purpose of creating a single unified company strategy around customer programs. Existing customer programs, which had been controlled by teams in individual countries and regions, were folded into the global framework. "Customer centricity" became the organization's new mantra.

But if Oracle was to become truly customer focused, it had to build better systems for listening to customers and gathering feedback in a comprehensive and consistent fashion. Through trial and error the team honed a globally unified customer-feedback platform. It was informed by data coming in from myriad "listening posts" that spanned the globe—everything from web surveys, focus groups, and executive-level advisory boards to marketplace studies and observations from individual employees interacting with customers.

One of the most effective feedback mechanisms was designed to take the pulse of a key constituency: chief information officers. Oracle's CIO Advisory Board has since become an indispensable source of guidance and a sounding board for new ideas. The board's message: Oracle needed to do a better job of coordinating resources and presenting a single voice—and a single ear—to the customer community. To a great extent, Oracle's global customer group became that singular interface.

Given the chance to speak, customers opened up. Their advice ran the gamut from recommendations on potential acquisitions to suggestions for improving account management, the latter becoming a recurring theme in a series of customer forums held during and after the PeopleSoft deal. Oracle needed a fresh account management approach, these customers said, one that would treat Oracle's biggest accounts in a more consistent and transparent fashion.

In response, Oracle's sales organization got busy retooling the company's account management practices. It crafted a new structure that placed senior executives in the role of overseeing high-priority accounts and actively helping with account planning and problem solving. At the same time, Oracle established a new "key account director" position that gave top customers a single point of contact for all things Oracle. Finally, the company formed an elite corps of "Oracle client advisors" who were charged with providing big-picture guidance to customers and helping flesh out new opportunities.

Customers applauded the restructuring move and welcomed the extra attention from Oracle executives. Issues got tackled faster and with fewer hassles. What's more, customers realized they could count on Oracle's account team for more than just handling sales orders and trouble tickets. Increasingly, Oracle reps were joining internal planning and strategy sessions—being treated in fact like an extension of the customer's own team.

Executive sponsorship and client advisors are just a couple examples of what Oracle calls "collaborative programs" that aim to build more strategic and fruitful partnerships with customers. Others include the Oracle President's Council, led by Oracle president Mark Hurd and board member Naomi Seligman. Collaboration also takes place through user groups involving hundreds of thousands of practitioners worldwide and through other customer-community-oriented programs.

From Transactions to Partnerships

To stay on track, Oracle now measures progress on a nearly constant basis. Every quarter Dasteel sits down with the top Oracle executives to talk progress and pore over performance numbers. Three topics are covered in each meeting. The first is customer satisfaction and loyalty. Second is "referenceability"—a customer's willingness to recommend Oracle—as measured by how many customers are actively participating in reference-based sales and marketing efforts. (Oracle today has more than 10,000 customers in this category.) Finally, the conversation turns to revenue impact. Every activity is measured against these three measures.

Higher levels of listening and collaboration have helped Oracle move the needle on customer relationships, replacing arms-length transactions with more intimate partnerships that can inspire additional business opportunities. Oracle regularly measures the continuum between both sides of this spectrum and tracks how incremental improvement in satisfaction and referencing drives further engagement and sales, especially for its top 2,000 customers. It has taken years for Oracle to get to this point—and more work lies ahead—but the effort is bearing fruit by helping customers innovate, become more agile and efficient, and get more impact from their IT investments.

Oracle's effort to get closer to customers would almost certainly fall short if the company didn't react in a meaningful way to feedback. "Customers get pretty frustrated if they don't see some corresponding response," Dasteel says, noting that Oracle makes a point of channeling relevant feedback into a set of "response programs" that are categorized as either one-to-one or one-to-many. The former typically involves an individual customer registering a complaint or service request through regular customer-support channels. The company's effectiveness in responding to these day-to-day technical issues is continually monitored.

Beyond this, the global customer team routinely sifts through the broader set of customer feedback, from the web surveys to the executive councils, and more recently even incorporating discussions on social media. The team strives to integrate all these channels and use Big Data analytical tools to uncover patterns and recurring themes that impact a large swath of the customer base. One effort is focused on linking reports of how customers "feel" about Oracle with their actual buying behavior.

All these examinations form the basis of the team's "Top 10 Program"—essentially a task force that tackles the most pressing issues affecting the largest portion of Oracle's customer base. The program mobilizes resources behind a response plan, which typically starts with communications to key customers and says, in effect, "We've listened, we've acted, this is what's changed, and here's how you can engage further." Exchanges also take place in small gatherings of customers, such as Oracle's President's Council and CIO Advisory Board, where Oracle executives sit down with customers and review their feedback, correlate it with the broader body of customer viewpoints, and explain what Oracle is doing about it. Similar conversations will take place with leaders of Oracle's huge user group community, and to reach even greater numbers, the team sends out electronic newsletters to update customers on hot topics.

Showing success in solving problems and correcting bad habits helps boost credibility with customers, who might otherwise turn a cold shoulder to Oracle's web surveys, forums, and other feedback-collection activities. "Customers would grow really tired of participating in those forums if they didn't feel like we were actually listening and doing something material about it," says Dasteel, who a few years ago was named Oracle's first chief customer officer (CCO).

In fact, Oracle's customer surveys report significant progress. From a relationship standpoint, customers say that Oracle is getting better at everything from coordinating resources and sharing best practices to serving as a trusted advisor. Tellingly, customers say they are happier with the latest releases of Oracle's products, in large part because their asked-for innovations—gathered by Oracle's feedback mechanisms—are routinely showing up in new products.

Oracle wisely transfers a large portion of this feedback into its CRM system, giving sales reps an accurate read on customers' emerging concerns and what Oracle is doing in response. Some reps have even signed up to get text alerts whenever new surveys come out. Executives say they want to set up similar connections with customers, the goal being to engage customers through their "channel of choice."

Today, Oracle is eager to engage in conversations on how to enhance the customer experience, a capability that is swiftly becoming a key differentiator for business. Says Oracle President Mark

Hurd, "Our customers are increasingly under the gun to innovate faster, and so much of that is customer-experience oriented. There is a clear competitive advantage in this, and we can be a significant help because it's foundational to what we're doing here at Oracle." Oracle executives say the critical lesson is that it's not about launching a single program or initiative, but more about changing a mindset; it is about making customer centricity part of the corporate DNA. What it comes down to is getting the entire company to listen to customers—and customers across industries confirm the shift. "In the last six or seven years, our relationship has evolved to one that is much more mature," said the CIO of a global manufacturer. "We've grown into a relationship that is much more strategic."

Customers also say their dealings with Oracle have become more collaborative, and brainstorming sessions are more common. "We have a different level of engagement with Oracle," says the CIO of a global construction and engineering firm. "Our conversations are more creative. We're more comfortable with throwing something at the wall to get their reaction. In the old world, they would say 'this does not fit with our product hierarchy,' but now it's likely to generate enthusiasm; the barriers have fallen away." Similarly, the CIO of a global airline says Oracle has "moved from building and selling a product to actually trying to help you learn how to take their products and innovate in your enterprise."

Oracle now ranks as one of the world's largest enterprise IT companies. In the past decade, it has doubled its market value and redefined the enterprise technology marketplace with innovations such as engineered systems, cloud services, and Big Data solutions. Would Oracle have made these advances if it had not also reinvented the daily experience of its customers—if it had not started listening? Most likely not. Thanks to its timely strategic recalibration and deliberate pursuit of a critical new business capability, Oracle is laying the groundwork for decades of market leadership.

How Oracle Drives Customer Centricity

To sustain growth and head off defections, Oracle radically reengineered the way it relates to customers. Here's how the database giant is turning around its reputation for turning off customers:

- **By setting up listening posts**—Oracle scours its customer base for opinions, launching web surveys, focus groups, and executive advisory boards to find out what it needs to do better.

- **By learning to collaborate**—Oracle's habit of dictating the terms of customer relationships was crimping growth. Now it fuels sales by becoming a sounding board for customers' ideas.

- **By moving beyond transactions**—In the early days, Oracle was all about racking up orders. Today, it's more likely to talk about enabling the customer's business.

- **By refocusing the sales teams**—To get customers' attention, Oracle restructured its sales organization, assigning top executives to key accounts and deploying strategic advisors to flesh out new customer opportunities.

- **By measuring progress**—Oracle leverages Big Data analytics to sort through customer feedback and link satisfaction measures with revenue growth.

9

Rockwell Embraces the Industrial Ethernet

Few companies have been innovating longer than Rockwell Automation. The world's largest industrial automation company has been turning out technology firsts for more than a hundred years. Rockwell's predecessor, Allen-Bradley, pioneered the nuts-and-bolts of motor control that controlled and powered manufacturing in the early twentieth century. Today, the Milwaukee-based Fortune 500 industrial automation powerhouse provides a new generation of software-enabled products that connect independent systems in manufacturing environments to make operations more productive.

Rockwell thrives on technological change but refrains from chasing every fad. Instead, it builds a consensus among its business and technology leaders before throwing its weight behind a technology trend. Once it settles on a strategy, however, Rockwell executes with precision and tenacity, which is how it has maintained its place as the leading player in the global market for industrial automation solutions.

A case in point: When Internet Protocol–based networks first made their appearance on factory floors, it wasn't obvious to Rockwell where the trend might lead. Until then, the Internet—and the Ethernet on which it is built—was confined to the front office, where enterprise planners used it to balance financial books and manage supply chains.

Out on the factory floor, however, the situation was different. A plethora of networks existed there, but they all ran on proprietary technologies that were essentially closed to the outside world. In fact, the idea of connecting factory floors or power plants to the Internet encountered a lot of resistance from engineers and business leaders.

"Fifteen years ago, there was a lot of pushback on that concept," says Sujeet Chand, Rockwell Automation's chief technology officer. Opponents argued that Ethernet networks weren't "deterministic" and thus incapable of real-time control over industrial operations. However, Rockwell's laboratories were proving otherwise. "We found that if you architected the Ethernet network correctly, you can get very good performance with standard, unmodified communication protocols that are used to power the Internet."

Smart Bet

Meanwhile, the cost of Ethernet was coming down, making it more attractive to manufacturers, oil and gas producers, and other industrial businesses. "We believed that as the cost of connectivity to Ethernet comes down, industrial automation systems would start adopting it more and more." Rockwell's business and technical leaders agreed and, in a major strategic move, decided that "the network to bet on" would be Ethernet.

Since then, Ethernet has become the fastest growing network used in the industrial automation market, forming the central nervous system of assembly lines and industrial process-control systems worldwide. Going with the Ethernet also synched with a larger business trend in which the worlds of IT and manufacturing—or office systems and plant floor networks—were coming together. The reason: New enterprise resource planning systems such as SAP and Oracle were rapidly spreading across corporate offices and changing how managers did everything, from financial accounting to buying raw materials.

In fact, Rockwell's customers were eager to integrate their manufacturing and business systems. Now they could quickly customize products to match incoming orders and adjust buying to meet factory-floor requirements. Integration would help Rockwell's customers speed deliveries and reduce waste. "We realized that we could drive costs lower by integrating functions that never tied together before," Rockwell's CTO Chand says. "Ethernet was the network that would really bring the two sides together."

Smart Devices

Rockwell's investment in the Ethernet brought the company face to face with the emerging Internet of Things—and it decided to capitalize on what it saw. The industrial company started designing a new generation of industrial devices, including sensors, actuators, and motor controllers that could be connected to standard Ethernet networks. These were the same networks consumers use to surf the Web—only ruggedized and secured to handle the tough conditions manufacturers and industrial companies face in real life.

Rockwell quickly found a profitable use for these Ethernet-enabled "smart" devices: helping companies monitor and manage their operations at a distance. "More and more customers want somebody to remotely monitor their assets and guarantee a certain uptime," Chand says. Energy producer Hilcorp, for instance, relies on Rockwell to keep an eye on its Alaskan oil fields from an office in Ohio. Special sensors in the oil rigs stream data to Rockwell technicians in Cleveland, who monitor the signals to spot trouble signs and avert equipment breakdowns.

M.G. Bryan, the Texas-based supplier of heavy equipment to oil and gas companies, is now outfitting its reservoir-fracturing pump trailers with Rockwell controllers, which continuously upload machine-performance data to the cloud. The new capability lets customers minimize downtime and cut costs via long-distance troubleshooting. Not surprisingly, orders for the trailers retrofitted with this "Internet of Things" feature are surging. Plus, M.G. Bryan says inbuilt usage monitoring allows it to attract new customers with innovative pay-by-use lease arrangements.

Rich Possibilities

Using machine data to watch over oil fields and factories only scratches the surface of what's possible when businesses embrace the Internet of Things. "Today we collect a lot of data, but it's often used to just open and close actuators or valves," Chand says. "There's a lot of data out there that's not being brought out over the Ethernet for analytics and other purposes."

That will change as industrial enterprises plug more and more machines into the Ethernet. Also helping is the rise of new technologies for collecting, sharing, and analyzing data in the cloud. "All this information can be collected in a cloud-level computing environment, where you can do a lot of analysis and modeling of this information," Chand says.

Big Data techniques, which facilitate rapid number crunching, will help businesses make short work of the masses of data generated by industrial systems. Rockwell hopes to harness all that information to do predictive analytics, advanced diagnostics, and other tasks that can give businesses an edge. From Rockwell's perspective, this is when the Internet of Things will really hit its stride.

Mobilizing for the Future

Rockwell's engineers have been testing some of these ideas. One promising application includes "active energy management" systems that can cut costs for heavy industrial users of the electrical grid. These systems employ smart devices and software agents to track energy usage and tweak production schedules to take advantage of periodic dips in utility rates. In industries such as cement production, where energy comprises a quarter of costs, the financial impact can be huge.

Chand believes we're on the cusp of the Internet of Things era, though more groundwork needs to be laid. Greater numbers of devices will need to become "smart" and enabled with sensors and Internet connectivity. (Cisco estimates that only 10 percent of devices are connected to the Ethernet today.) And with terabytes of sensitive data traveling between industrial operations and the cloud, the industry will need to invest more in cyber defenses.

What's more, businesses will need new technical standards to help make sense of all the smart machine data. "If every single device starts transmitting information, you need a way to sort through and classify that information, figure out what's useful, and throw away what's not," Chand says. "The amount of logic that needs to be built for that is pretty significant, so developing standards around machine-generated information will be critical."

Rockwell won't be alone in tackling these technical challenges. A network of partners will supply key enabling technologies, such as hardware for intelligently transmitting information over industrial networks. To that end, Rockwell has forged a partnership with Cisco, the world's leading maker of Internet switches and routers.

Rockwell's bet on the Ethernet has given the company a head start in a market poised for massive growth. In the last decade, as factories have been installing standard Internet Protocol networks at record pace, Rockwell has bolstered its product lineup with cloud connectivity capabilities. Most of the motor controllers it makes these days come with cloud plug-in options, and if demand keeps expanding as expected, such gateways to the Internet of Things may become a standard feature.

Rockwell's chief technologist sees no slowdown in the proliferation of smart devices, which will pour ever-greater volumes of information into global networks. "Given the fact that devices are getting smarter, Ethernet is becoming pervasive, and with the advent of cloud computing, the amount of information that most business leaders will have is going to grow exponentially."

Business leaders, he says, will need to figure out what these trends mean to them. "They need to determine what they can get from the Internet of Things that could change business models, that could change the way they're doing business," Chand says. And he advises businesses to get ready for a new wave of innovation. "If they don't capitalize on it, they're going to miss a major opportunity." From Rockwell's perspective, things are just starting to get interesting. For Rockwell, this is the early stage of this journey. Industry adoption and innovation will start accelerating going forward.

Part IV
Governance

10

Tough Rules for Tough Times

Ruthless Execution Checklist

- Do you regularly brief your board members regarding customer successes and customer value delivered?
- Is customer success a regular part of the board's agenda?
- Are your top executives and board members meeting with customers on a regular basis to ensure you're meeting their changing needs?
- Are board members and executives conversant in your company's major technology initiatives?
- Does the board play a role in shaping how emerging technology trends such as cloudification and Big Data can advance the strategic goals of the organization?

So far this book has covered in detail two of the three strategies that business leaders need to employ to break through the wall: leadership and critical capabilities. In this chapter, we will discuss the third essential strategy: governance. By **governance**, we mean the set of rules that allow companies to ensure that their strategies and actions will lead to business success.

We divide governance into two broad areas. One falls within the purview of a company's executive leadership, including the board of directors, and involves establishing high-level oversight of a company's most important investments and strategic initiatives. The other has to do with operational governance, which includes the practices and systems that corporate leaders put in place to ensure accountability and results. We will share our findings and recommendations on this part of governance in the next chapter.

New Rules for the Board

One of the outcomes of the great recession is a higher standard being placed on the board of directors. Today, the board needs to be responsible for more than just setting direction—it must also hold the executive team accountable for carrying out these strategies.

In the chapters on leadership, you saw that business leaders decided what strategies should be employed to induce a business recovery or stay ahead of their competition. We outlined a simple and proven strategic recalibration process that unifies and focuses the board and the company on the few, critical activities to meet their long-term goals. We discussed the advent of a new corporate performance metric called the **return on strategy** (ROS), which aligns investment decisions, resources, and capital by weighing factors that are specific to a company's strategy. We then presented a corporate planning process that incorporates ROS in the portfolio planning process and drives execution of the strategy. The board plays a key role in facilitating the development of these practices and must hold the CEO accountable should these practices fail to be integrated into the culture of the company.

Next, in the critical capabilities section, we reviewed a portfolio of recalibrating actions that businesses need to carry out to successfully overcome rude awakenings and lay the groundwork for continued growth. In the past, these actions have included finding and keeping talented individuals, acquiring companies that bring strategic advantage, and rigorously managing productivity.

We believe these capabilities remain crucial to business success today and should be top of mind not just for CEOs and other executive managers, but for every board member as well. The good news is that directors and senior executives by and large do exemplary work in these areas. The best boards play an active role in building a strong bench of future leaders to succeed the current generation, and they routinely step up to conduct sensitive consultations and make tough calls when senior executives fail to perform as expected, or lose the confidence of top customers and investors. Board members also do a good job stepping up when the company is weighing or executing a major transaction, such as purchasing another company.

In this chapter, we propose that boards and senior leadership need to pay attention to two new critical capabilities we outlined earlier in the last chapter—namely, customer success management and the cloudification of business. In the past, boards of directors and leadership teams have given short shrift to both of these areas. But the plain truth is that boards and senior leaders can no longer afford to overlook these capabilities if they expect the companies they govern to win during a time when customer expectations are higher than ever before.

Boards and Customer Success

We saw in our analysis of business-software leader Oracle that companies can run into trouble if they don't invest in the success of their customers in an era of increasing customer empowerment. Facing a skeptical base of customers brought in by acquisition, Oracle initiated a concerted effort to start listening to their concerns, and then responded effectively with improved business practices and better products so that customers would gain maximum value from their purchases. Diligent collection and analysis of feedback and ongoing communications to customers were core to this initiative, which has effectively turned around customers' perception of the Oracle brand.

Prominent in this effort were Oracle leaders who stepped up their outreach to influential customers, calming their nerves and slowly building loyalty. Oracle board member Naomi Seligman, for example, teamed with President Mark Hurd to form Oracle President's Council to build more productive relationships with top customers. In our view, companies would greatly benefit by enlisting board members in similar customer-focused programs.

We believe customer success should become a corporate imperative that engages top leadership in a systematic way. Goals of this initiative should include targeted communications that tell customers you are serious about listening and realigning operations and products to meet their evolving needs. Moreover, board members should actively interrogate senior executives on the real value customers are capturing from their company's products and services.

Above all, board members and executive leadership should sharpen their focus on assessing and communicating the business value that customers are realizing from their investments. The most critical components of this effort should be included on the agenda of board meetings and key analyst consultations, and in the company's annual report. Appropriate members of your board should be tasked with visiting leading customers at least once a year and getting frank and evidence-based assessments of the value your products are delivering. For customer success to truly become part of your corporate DNA, and for customers to take your efforts seriously, board members and senior leaders must make it clear that this is an issue that is at the top of their minds and that key stakeholders need to have skin in the game.

Boards' Clouded View

In our discussion of leadership, we identified a major shortcoming in the ranks of those who are entrusted with guiding companies through trying times: Most boards and their partners in the executive suite simply lack the necessary technical expertise—or even a fundamental appreciation for technology—to comprehend a majority of the investments their businesses are making. This in spite of the monumental technology-induced shifts that are disrupting industries, including the "cloudification of business" discussed earlier in the book, and the increasing "commoditization" of IT that is seeing businesses scramble to give employees and customers the same easy online experiences they're used to at home.

In light of this, one might have expected a corresponding increase in the board's attention to technology issues. Surely more and more directors would be seeking out chief information officers and top technologists for information and advice. Wouldn't you expect these experts to be routine presenters at board meetings? Not so.

In our interviews with directors, we found that most see IT merely as the cost of doing business. In most cases, they discounted IT's strategic role and even questioned whether IT should be expected to yield a measurable ROI. Our own research found that less than 12 percent of companies measure the value of their IT investments. Although business executives may recognize the importance of IT investments, they are missing opportunities by not measuring that value and paying close attention to IT's contributions to innovation.

One former CEO, now the chairman of a global technology company, told us he was very disappointed that technology is still seen as the cost of doing business instead of as a strategic weapon. He added that boards haven't changed the way they govern IT in more than 20 years, and he was surprised there hasn't been more education and involvement by boards in IT. "Board members these days are more concerned about avoiding lawsuits...than they are in thinking strategically about making the company win in the marketplace," he told us.

This highlights a troubling reality: The vast majority of boards are unaware of the value the organization is deriving from its technology investments—this despite the enormous sums that are routinely spent on large-scale software implementations, "cloud" initiatives, data centers, and so on. Indeed, it is not uncommon for companies to spend more than 50 percent of their capital budget on IT, and in some industries that percentage can be upwards of 75%. "How can you possibly know if your IT spend is appropriate?" the former CIO of a Fortune 500 company told us.

In fact, we found that boards and CEOs frequently do keep tabs on the very largest IT projects, but superficially asking only about whether projects are on budget and schedule. They neglect to ask the larger question of whether the project is worth the investment in the first place. One board member told us his company had spent more than a billion dollars on an ERP implementation but he had no idea how much value they've gotten from it.

We heard similar stories from other executives whose firms took huge risks and sank billions into computing systems. Although directors may have demanded regular progress reports from the CIO, they never bothered to ask about the expected "returns." Huge risks are also left unaddressed, such as threats from data breaches or cyber attacks, which beg serious attention from senior leadership.

Clearly changes are needed in how boards and top corporate executives deal with information technology and its potential impact on the health and future direction of the business. Boards should be asking the same tough, value-oriented questions that the CEO and CFO should be asking:

- Are our technology investments paying off?

- How can technology advance the strategic goals of the organization?

- How can we take advantage of the cloudification of business to create new products, services, and associated pricing models?

- What can we learn from other companies, customers, and vendors and their investments in the business cloud?

- In what ways should our operating and governance model adapt to support these changes?

In the next chapter, we'll outline sound policies and practices that enable leaders to properly frame the rules of the game before they put these strategies into practice.

11

Achieving Operational Excellence

In the previous chapter we showed how corporate boards acting in concert with senior executives can help businesses embrace critical new capabilities around customer success and the cloudification of businesses. In the leadership section, we outlined how business leaders focus their business strategies through an integrated strategy-to-execution process. With these constructs in place, a company has the playing field lined up and ready for play. Now we want to focus on how leaders can set up the rules of the game by embracing three important elements: accountability, performance management, and discipline.

Accountability

To manage through turbulent times and performance walls, leaders must develop a strong system of accountability. Not only must they know what tasks to assign, they must also make sure that senior colleagues take responsibility for getting those tasks implemented efficiently, speedily, and precisely as designed. And most important, they must deliver results.

Nothing is more important to a smoothly run organization than having a solid system of accountability. By **accountability**, we mean not just personal accountability, but accountability that deals with the greater good of the company—moving away from what's good for your particular part of the business to what is best for the overall company. This is something that business leaders struggle with the most.

Most business leaders use the "team" word in their rhetoric. However, the real challenge is to truly get senior leaders to think and act to maximize their company's return on strategy, even at the expense of their individual business areas.

Accountability is nothing more than making good on one's commitments, goals, and targets, and dealing with the consequences if one does not keep those commitments. This might sound "ruthless," but when this message is effectively communicated, as it was with the leaders we studied, it will come off sounding fair and clear, and will be respected by the greater organization.

How can one guarantee that executives will feel the need to be accountable? That brings us to our next practice under governance: the performance management system.

Performance Management System

If accountability is about making good on one's promises, goals, and targets, the single best way to make sure that employees are accountable is to put in place the best possible system for measuring results. Just as a company must have a smoothly working accountability system to break through a wall, it is just as critical that it have an effective performance management system.

A proper performance management system helps employees learn what is important, how tasks are to be measured, and how those tasks affect the overall business enterprise. It can become an effective tool for aligning management and employees as they seek to attain targeted goals. It can show business leaders how to go from broad strategies to day-to-day actions. It can transmit a company's strategies not just to the top leadership, but throughout the company.

An effective performance management system helps communicate goals and strategies, providing management the understanding to create a true performance-focused organization. It permits business leaders to measure actual performance against the full potential of their businesses. Not surprisingly, research indicates that companies with strong performance management systems do better than their peers.

What performance management systems should be used to deal with rude awakenings in your business? Most companies in the past have determined their financial progress by looking at benchmarks such as sales, margins, profit, and market value. But to truly judge the strategic welfare of a company, you need performance management systems that reflect the entire strategy of the company—how customers look at the value proposition.

Results or Bust

Unfortunately, most companies' strategic priorities were often entirely separated from the way employees were evaluated and the tasks those employees were asked to perform. As a result, a company's most strategic projects were often run by people who had capacity instead of the top performers in the organization.

The business leaders we studied have done whatever it takes to avoid a situation in which they have had to explain away bad results. They learned that they had to put in place rewards and incentive systems that helped to ensure that employees would deliver on what mattered to the company. An effective performance management system makes sure that results get delivered and that the results are for the good of the company.

An effective system of performance measurement requires the following tasks:

- Identifying and correctly benchmarking key business performance metrics

- Planning business activities with operating measurements in mind

- Creating a technical capability that will gather, store, and support the measurement process

Most companies struggle constantly with performance measurement. They create performance management systems that are overly complicated. An effective system must be simple, transparent, and uniform—one that will greatly aid others in understanding your company's strategies, and truly reflect how the company creates value.

Not All Measures Are Created Equal

Business leaders often do not differentiate between using different kinds of performance measures, but they should.

Metric Discrimination

Business leaders should not use the same kinds of measures to gauge different kinds of business initiatives. For example, they should use certain measures to track growth activity and other measures for activities designed simply to run the business.

The performance portfolio framework shown in Table 11-1 depicts how business leaders should discriminate between various performance measures. For example, some measures are much more appropriate when you are in a growth mode than when you are in a performance mode. And sometimes measures are available that are not used but can provide valuable insight.

Table 11-1   Risk/Reward Calibrator

Portfolio Type	Risk	Payback Period	Return Type
Run the Business	Low	3–12 months	SG&A (sales, general and administrative)
Improve the Business	Medium to high	12–24 months	Margin; working capital improvement
Grow the Business	Medium to high	12–36 months	Core and new revenue growth
Innovate the Business	Low to medium	24–36 months	Revenue growth and new business offerings

As we show in our upcoming study of industry-leader Banfield Pet Hospital, one of the most critical steps to driving company performance was the CEO's revamp of performance measurements and accountability across his leadership team. By developing an effective set of corporate performance measures—along with fair systems of accountability—the company was able to better align the workforce with corporate objectives, all the way to the store level. The results have been truly transformational, with the company doubling revenues over the past five years while markedly improving customer satisfaction.

Walking the Tightrope

The measurement problem is typically bimodal. Either companies measure the right things but don't do a good job of actually measuring and tracking, or they measure too many things, many of which aren't relevant. Getting this right is a delicate balancing act.

Some business initiatives lend themselves to easily quantifiable measures such as cost savings. Others rely on revenue and profit growth, especially those initiatives that cover new markets or incremental revenue opportunities. Still others are measured by nonfinancial factors such as improved customer experience, better customer-facing processes, and increasing the value of a product or service to the customer.

A performance management system must be context specific: The business leader first decides what business initiative to undertake, and then makes sure there is an appropriate mechanism to review and track that initiative.

On the performance side, measures should be much more attuned to short-term revenue growth (for example, return on invested capital). The left side of the portfolio framework lends itself better to traditional kinds of performance measures: It includes discounted cash flow analysis and ROI calculations.

As for right-side growth initiatives, ROI measures simply don't work. Breakthroughs and rational experimentations or seeds of growth are the hallmark of this part of the portfolio. These kinds of initiatives often deal with emerging investments, where the disparity between the potential upside and downside is large, future revenues are highly uncertain, and initial investments are relatively small compared to the requisite future investments of scaling fully. Also, time horizons are longer than usual.

Although companies would never play fast and loose with performance measures when it comes to their core business, they often take a nonchalant view of performance measurement when it comes to the growth side. Many business leaders tend to be less rigorous when it comes to measuring growth efforts. Why is that?

One reason is that executives interested in growth projects tend to change strategies so rapidly that it becomes too difficult to think of either a long-term strategy or a measure that follows from the strategy. Another reason is that measurement is resource intensive. Acquiring performance measurement data sometimes requires large amounts of capital investment and human resources. Finally, executives interested in growth-oriented initiatives tend to rely on measures that are soft; however, the investment community does not put much value in soft measures. Wall Street has had a high comfort level with hard numbers—revenues and margins—but when it comes to the softer measures dealing with things such as customer perception, the data is not so highly valued.

Executives engaged in right-side business now express financial performance not so much in terms of GAAP measures (which focus on present-period costs and revenues), but more on prospective valuations that reflect growth platforms.

With regard to performance management, here are the key principles used by the successful business leaders we studied:

- **Principle 1:** They focus on a select few performance measurements and take great care not to dilute the need for focus with too many measures. It is critical to find measures that matter to the business. Ask yourself, what is the total number of metrics you and your managers track? How many of those metrics are truly relevant to shareholder value?

- **Principle 2:** They believe that an unusually broad set of measures slows down execution and complicates rather than clarifies the critical managerial discussions and decision making required. To these leaders, driving shareholder value is their number-one priority. All other measures come second.

- **Principle 3:** They prefer certain operating measures, such as top-line revenue growth, cash flow, working capital reduction, and return on invested capital, as the key performance indicators that will drive shareholder value.

- **Principle 4:** They are relentless about determining what performance measures truly matter and make sure that those performance measures are linked to the strategic priorities of the company. Unfortunately, as you move down in an organization, you will find that often more than 50 percent of the metrics being used have little relevance to company results.

- **Principle 5:** They prefer performance measurement systems that are disciplined and rigorous. A system is disciplined when the measurement and review processes are applied consistently and fairly on a regular basis and that "gaming the system" is minimized.

- **Principle 6:** They make a habit of revisiting these performance measurements every year to prevent them from getting stale or becoming obsolete. It is amazing how long leaders can go without truly questioning the currency and relevance of the numbers they manage by.

- **Principle 7:** Because they are fact based in their approach to performance measurement, they are comfortable setting stretch goals. In most companies, target setting is a joke.

- **Principle 8:** They have a clear focus on what business initiatives really matter and only measure results.

- **Principle 9:** They are careful not to employ performance measures and targets blindly across the business.

- **Principle 10:** They adopt measures that are very actionable, clearly and easily communicated across the organization, and, most important, controllable and relevant to peoples' day-to-day activities.

In deciding how and why to allocate resources to the four quadrants of the portfolio framework, it makes sense to account for differences in terms of risk, payback period, and return type, as shown in Table 11-1.

In summary, there are good reasons for business leaders to build strong performance measurement systems as part of their recovery efforts. If those systems are clear and precise, they can help align individual objectives, departmental functional goals, and company-wide strategic efforts.

Discipline

In addition to effective accountability and performance management systems, business leaders have found that discipline is an important "rule of the game" in bouncing back from business reversals.

Discipline means, above all else, knowing what has to be done, and making sure it gets done with consistency and rigor. For companies that are not mature, this is a difficult transition.

In a previous chapter, we discussed a transformational story of business-software leader Oracle. Its dedication over the past decade to developing a customer-centric culture led to tremendous results. To create this paradigm shift for a company the size of Oracle, leadership had to be very disciplined in the design, rollout, and ongoing support for the program.

Discipline is all about getting results. Discipline drives consistency, the timeliness of decisions, and the institutionalizing of a formal process. In these ways, discipline is tied to performance management.

Executives who want to drive discipline through the organization had better be disciplined themselves. Employees aren't going to mind working in a disciplined manner, but they have no incentive to work hard, to work creatively, or to work efficiently if they find that the boss is not.

Rigor is important to the whole notion of discipline. To be rigorous and establish discipline, there must be a system of rewards and consequences that is based on facts and analytical depth.

The Discipline of Capital Investment

The budget is the bane of corporate America.... Making a budget is an exercise in minimalization. You're always trying to get the lowest out of your people....

—Jack Welch (*Fortune* magazine)

Inextricably tied to effective strategic recalibration and performance management is everyone's favorite annual exercise: the budget process. It is amazing how long companies force their people to spend on an activity that is so dreaded (for a company of any reasonable size, it is not uncommon for this process to take six months or more). From our vantage point, anything more than 60 days is obscene. Nonetheless, most organizations have a budgeting process that is fraught with problems:

- The capital investment process often breeds a sense of entitlement throughout the organization. It encourages "use it or lose it" behavior, which forces poor decision making for fear of not getting unused funds back.

- The calendar and financial focus of the process inhibits the understanding of performance issues.

- The typically centralized effort encourages resource silos and binds those resources to particular organizations rather than allowing them to move to new priorities.

- The procedure is typically long on process and details and short on valuable information business leaders require to run the business.

- The yearly effort and the allocation process do not leave room for priorities or opportunities that come up during off-cycle periods, and many investment/project opportunities are indeed off-cycle.

From Capital Management to Strategic Investment

It is squarely on the shoulders of the CFO to fix these issues. More than anyone else, the CFO holds the key to linking the strategic planning and recalibration effort and the capital- and resource-allocation process. Companies that excel at this lean toward a more frequent and shorter effort, which provides them with more accurate forecasts and a more flexible allocation of funds.

Striving for Consistency

Smart business executives, in their quest for discipline, need to reward the kind of behavior that contributes to the results they are seeking. If it's teamwork that is being sought, then reward team performance, not individual performance. If it's superior customer service, don't reward volume and nothing else.

Establishing discipline does not mean punishing every employee who makes a mistake. Employees should be permitted to make mistakes without the bosses coming down on them harshly each time. Achieving desired results may require experimentation, gambling on something not tried before. Therefore, mistakes are going to occur. They are inevitable. Think of any employee who makes mistakes as gaining the kind of experience that prevents mistakes in the future. That's a kind of discipline, too.

Nothing is more important than being consistent in passing on messages. Employees are going to search hard for reasons not to make the extra effort that leads to sought-after results. No one wants to waste time and effort. Therefore, consistent messaging avoids the impression that management has no idea what to do.

However, even knowing how to execute does not guarantee that companies will be able to impose discipline easily. Companies, especially those that are doing well, find it hard to rein in employees who have been told that the main goal of the company is to grow.

We have seen that the three elements mentioned prominently in this chapter—accountability, performance management, and discipline—are the building blocks with respect to governance. However, commitment and compliance are essential for the new rules of the game to work. By **commitment**, we mean up and down buy-in to the new rules of the game. By **compliance**, we mean actual conformity and adherence to the new rules. Everyone must be on board, especially the senior leadership team.

In the next chapter, we show how one company has transformed itself from a niche-market player into a national presence with category-leading profitability. It has done this largely by recalibrating its governance structures and establishing innovative accountability systems. To every pet owner, the health of their companion is of upmost importance. Banfield Pet Hospitals has taken this to heart by focusing on proactive healthcare for animals. That focus on delivering superior care, and the importance it has on the success of the company, is made clear through governance practices that have become drivers of the company's success.

12

The Discipline of Change: Banfield Pet Hospital

As recent economic upheavals remind us, change remains the only constant for the majority of businesses today. We are in a business climate that calls out for creative leadership and fresh business philosophies to steer companies through the deep organizational and cultural shifts needed to propel long-term growth. A prime example is Banfield Pet Hospital, the largest privately owned veterinary practice in the U.S., with more than 850 clinics in the U.S., Puerto Rico, and Mexico.

Founded in 1955, Banfield has grown from a single clinic in Portland, Oregon to current market leadership because it pursued a different business model in an industry traditionally populated by "mom and pop" pet clinics. The company has stuck to its vision, methodically pursuing operational efficiency in the face of cultural and structural inertia that would have stymied most businesses. According to analyst reports, Banfield is a billion-dollar company.

Managers had little reason to worry about running a nationwide chain during Banfield's early years. The pet hospital's founder Warren Wegert was focused on perfecting a single veterinary practice in northeast Portland, Oregon. Naming his clinic after the nearby Banfield Freeway, Wegert's clinic attracted a loyal clientele of area pet owners and brought in revenue of about $2 million per year.

In 1987, Wegert sold the clinic to entrepreneur Scott Campbell. The new owner teamed up with pet store chain PetSmart in 1994 to open "VetSmart" clinics in their stores; and in 1999, Banfield purchased PetSmart's remaining clinics, growing the chain further. In 2007, Campbell sold additional shares of the company to both PetSmart and Mars, Incorporated. Though Mars is best known as a leading global food manufacturer, it is also the world's largest pet food manufacturer. Following the transaction, the management reins were turned over to a new CEO, John Payne, who previously ran Bayer Animal Health. Under Payne's direction, and despite the economic crisis of 2008, the company was named one of 13 companies that would be hiring in 2009.

Banfield's journey from a single clinic to national network presented distinct challenges for the pet clinic network, including its unrelenting focus on preventive care for pets. Banfield was and continues to be a leader in the preventive care movement, something other veterinary practices are just now beginning to embrace.

The company was moving from an entrepreneurial venture in which the founder made all the key decisions to a multiunit enterprise where decision making and accountability would be distributed at various levels across the organization. To leverage the scale economies of a national operation and boost same-store earnings, the new Banfield would need to implement a greater degree of financial and operational discipline and deploy more standardized operational processes both at the corporate level and across the veterinary clinic network.

Tony Ueber joined Banfield as chief operating officer in 2009 and was named president and chief executive officer in 2012. A graduate of UCLA's Anderson School of Business, Ueber came with deep connections to the retail and healthcare industries, having spent six years at Office Depot in executive positions and before that at McKinsey's healthcare practice. Ueber's background in multiunit retailing gave the new CEO a head start in leading Banfield's sprawling network. But there were critical differences that made the pet hospital a tough venture to lead.

Although the pet hospital shares the outward characteristics of a traditional retail chain—the company's distinctive logo greets customers at all 850 locations—Banfield in many ways is a one-of-a-kind operation, and the marketplace offers few templates for success. Unlike its retailing partner PetSmart, or its parent and consumer packaged goods leader Mars, Incorporated, Banfield is at its heart a medical services business serving pets and their owners and deals with higher levels of uncertainty and variability on a routine basis, from new puppy visits to emergency services. As a result, the pet hospital's business model is riskier—one that eventually called for a new organizational structure, including a novel dual-leadership model of medicine and operations and a rigorous performance management process spanning every level of the organization.

Contrast Banfield with a traditional retail chain: No matter what the skills and expertise the store manager may have, at the end of the day he or she works with roughly the same physical layout, and key parameters of the business are centrally controlled, including merchandising, pricing, point-of-sale materials, and so on. Banfield is different.

In its 2000-square-foot hospitals, Banfield provides a wide range of services to clients and their pets, including X-rays, lab work, emergency care, and surgeries.

"We offer a far more complex range of services than a retailer," Ueber says. "We partner with clients and their pets for their life-long care. It's a much deeper relationship than your average retail transaction."

Making matters tougher is the composition of Banfield's work-force—a mix of more than 2,900 salaried veterinary doctors and a diverse supporting staff of more than 13,000 technicians and business administrators. Intelligently motivating this blend of talent and back-grounds was a critical component of Banfield's new business philosophy. "We have this very diverse, widely dispersed group of associates that we needed to bond around a common vision and culture," Ueber says.

Banfield sought to preserve the integrity and independence of its medical professionals while simultaneously enacting new business processes that would enable clinics to get more nimble and efficient, make quicker decisions, and grow profitability. Banfield's strategy also focused on driving satisfying experiences for customers and their pets. This would take a combination of excellent doctors, improved preventive care programs, and consistently pleasing clinic visits. Ultimately, Ueber wanted to replicate great customer experiences in addition to improved health outcomes at each one of Banfield's 850-plus clinics.

Getting Buy-In

Leadership at Banfield knew that any change of course would need commitment from their veterinarians. "Our whole business hinges on the doctors and the quality of care we provide," Ueber says. "Practicing quality medicine is the heart of our business, and our doctors put medicine first, which is quite different than retail managers."

The Banfield leadership team needed to find a way to bring two cultures together: operations and medicine. They needed their veterinary doctors to understand they were part of a larger operation and a bigger mission, and they needed their operations staff to understand the complexity of medical services.

"Veterinarians often enter their careers with the concept and notion they will be working in one hospital," Ueber says. "We had the challenge of making them feel a part of 850 hospitals and the immense benefits that brings from a medical research and resources perspective, to know that they're part of a $13-billion global pet care business. And beyond that, to feel they're part of Mars, Incorporated, a $35 billion, 70,000-employee company."

Other challenges included dispelling traditional notions of how medical clinics should work. For example, early in its history, Banfield was the first pet clinic to develop a preventive care approach for pets and deliver it consistently across the practice through an efficient back-office structure. After seeing the medical results and how they can use Banfield's size and scale to make a true difference in the industry and the profession with their knowledge and research, Banfield doctors embrace and continue to lead the preventive care model. Banfield doctors also understand the necessity of business efficiency, which meant adopting a new set of operating principles. "One of the reasons why we've been able to thrive when others haven't is our unwavering focus on preventive care coupled with operational performance and efficiency," Ueber says.

Ueber started by building a leadership team equally committed to operational and medical excellence. This was critical to accelerating the cultural shift required for success, and Ueber was keen to ensure quality medical care would not suffer from its commitment to efficiency.

Banfield's management team also worked to develop a unique model for quality of care for its practice by looking at human medicine best practices.

In fact, studies show that as medical clinics become more efficient, quality of care rises, in part because practitioners make fewer mistakes. In the case of a pet hospital network such as Banfield, it means that pets wait less time to be seen, staff move pets in and out of kennels fewer times, pets experience less stress, and the odds of miscommunication leading to medical mistakes are diminished. "You get better medical outcomes when your pets are under less anxiety or less stress," Ueber says.

Yet, it would be no easy task to bridge the cultures between Banfield's medical and business professionals. Ueber found this out early on when he launched a cross-functional team (consisting of doctors and business managers) to forge a commitment behind transforming the business. "It was challenging at times, "Ueber said. "Bringing two cultures together, medicine and operations, in a way that has never been done before was a huge undertaking for the entire company."

To help build a new consensus, Ueber reorganized the top management structure. In the process, Banfield learned a valuable lesson in organizational design—namely that changing the DNA and solidifying new ways of thinking takes constant reinforcement over an extended period of time. "The biggest learning for me was just how long it takes to affect culture. You have to be very intentional about where you're going and make sure you're constantly reinforcing behaviors that you desire." The Banfield executive team solidified the company's direction using classic portfolio management techniques. After identifying the most promising initiatives, the leaders drew up a multiyear plan to execute the strategy and established performance management systems to track progress against specific goals.

Monkey Business: The Five Monkeys Experiment

"We've always done it that way" is the common refrain you hear in too many organizations. In fact, resistance to change is one of the biggest impediments to breaking through performance barriers. So why do people cling to old habits when there's a better way available? The story of the five monkeys may explain why.

As recounted by Gary Hamel and C. K. Prahalad in their book *Competing for the Future*, the story goes like this: An experimenter puts five monkeys in a large cage. In the center of the cage is a tall pole with a bunch of bananas suspended from the top. One of the five monkeys scampers up the pole and grabs the bananas. Just as he does, the experimenter blasts the monkey with a torrent of cold water. The monkey runs back down the pole without the bananas. Eventually, the other four try it with the same outcome. Finally, the monkeys just sit and don't even try again.

But then, one of the monkeys is removed and replaced with a new one. The new monkey enters the room, spots the bananas and decides to go for it. Just as he is about to scamper up the pole, the other four reach out and drag him back down. After a while, he gets the message. There is something wrong or bad that happens if you go after those bananas. Experimenters kept replacing an existing monkey with a new one, and each time none of the new monkeys ever made it to the top. They each got the same message. Don't climb that pole. None of them knew exactly why they shouldn't climb the pole, they just knew not to. In other words, "We've always done it that way around here."

Overcoming cultural inertia was one of the toughest challenges Banfield faced as it sought to transform its pet hospital business. Through clear communications, constant reinforcement of new roles and responsibilities, and rigorous performance measurement, the organization succeeded in changing entrenched mindsets that had been slowing progress.

Breaking Barriers

Armed with a clear strategy, Banfield executives proceeded to break down barriers and rally the medical and business staff behind a common cause. Informing their business plan with organizational design practices from the retail industry, the management team restructured the hospital chain's organizational chart. The initiative paired a team of business-focused field directors with a parallel group of medical directors. Their shared goal: driving quality of care and consistency across the chain. If executed correctly, Banfield would be able to reap synergies and scale out of the best practices of both business and medicine and thus provide invaluable benefits to the industry and the profession.

Banfield had previously fielded a team of district managers, with each district manager overseeing as many as 60 or 70 hospitals. In Banfield's view, the team was stretched too thin to exert any real oversight over individual clinics. "With a span of control that big, you can't implement any initiatives or process changes." The most you can do is "come in with a checklist and a white glove and do inspections, or come in and just drop off donuts and say hi to everybody," commented Ueber.

Consequently, one of the new Banfield teams' first projects was to reduce the span of control to approximately 15 hospitals, which gave Banfield the leverage it needed to drive efficiency initiatives and operational accountability while continuing its commitment to quality care. Bolstering the field organization added a layer of cost, but the move would pay for itself with the proceeds from operating efficiencies and staff productivity.

Banfield then instituted a unique performance management process (drawing on a technique developed by parent Mars, Incorporated) that evaluates a broader range of staff than is usual for the profession, including everyone from top medical and business executives to frontline staff such as veterinary assistants. For Banfield, it was critical to set clear expectations with every associate and hold people accountable. To track progress against medical, customer, and associate staffing goals, the company created the equivalent of a "strategic scorecard."

Next, Banfield changed how its business managers relate to its doctors, and took steps to ensure that business directors gave doctors the respect they deserved. "We made sure business and medical staffs were equal partners," Ueber says. "For some field directors this meant unlearning old patterns of thinking tied to conventional retail settings."

Banfield's partnership approach called for a new kind of business manager, one that understands the mindset of a medical professional. "Finding operational managers who can relate to doctors, who appreciate what doctors bring to the practice, and understand their language and terminology, is really critical," Ueber says.

Ideally, Banfield would also be able to hire doctors who possessed an equal measure of business savvy, allowing every clinic to be run by a medical director who also had a head for operations. Tight labor markets, however, called for a modified approach. Concluding that it would be unlikely the company could find enough veterinarians with a strong business background, Ueber put in place what he calls a "dual leadership model." Today, Banfield's clinicians "report up" through the company's medical field team; business directors do the same through the operations team. Partnerships between medical and business directors crisscross the structure, but the two lines ultimately converge at the Banfield management team.

Banfield's novel strategy—reinforced by clear leadership and accountability—has paid off by giving the company superior operational control. Synching business and medical teams has been a "huge enabler," Ueber says, driving more nimble decision making and allowing the different locations to make faster decisions and improve the quality of medical care at any given location. Moreover, the resulting market momentum is attracting better talent to work at Banfield's clinics. Meanwhile, having better accountability and discipline at the business level has been key to the success of growing quality service innovations, such as discounted preventive care packages called Optimum Wellness Plans, and has guided the company's fresh brand strategy, which includes a new package of marketing programs.

Banfield's transformation from a neighborhood clinic to a global-scale medical provider is generating clear rewards. Last year, Banfield increased its comparable same-store sales by a double-digit percentage and saw a similar boost this year. These are unprecedented levels of store-based growth for the industry. In the past five years the business has gone from under $500 million in revenue to a billion. "The rest of the profession now is looking at us and going, 'Wow, these guys seem to be doing pretty well and making a huge difference in the pet care world.' And many are starting to follow a similar path of focusing on preventive care, client experience, and operational excellence," Ueber said.

Banfield demonstrates that effective governance coupled with bold leadership can radically transform a business in an industry with no ready-made formulas for success. Crucial to this achievement: the ability of leaders to tie strategy to execution by means of a well-defined performance management process, which includes holding associates accountable. In a traditionally fragmented market characterized by small operators, Banfield is pioneering a business model that leverages scale and efficiencies to deliver both outstanding pet care and business success.

Part V
What It All Means

13

Final Thoughts

Hitting the wall and managing through tough times *has* become a new business norm. Business cycles continue to compress, historical barriers to entry are being removed with technology innovation, regulatory scrutiny has intensified, and global macro-economic gyrations wreak havoc on long-term planning. All of these external factors are keeping our business leaders up at night as they try to navigate through ever-choppy waters. This book has attempted to present a practical and proven approach on how to maintain a path of success and how businesses can recover after *hitting performance walls*. Our hope is that after reading this book, you will have the fundamental business principles and operational practices to succeed in today's marketplace.

As this book shows, many of the biggest companies in the business world have hit the wall. With strong leadership and innovative business practices, these companies have figured out how to reposition their companies for growth with critical capabilities such as customer centricity and cloud-enabled business opportunities. These successful leaders are highlighted in this book because they have navigated through turbulent times and broken through performance walls.

It's never easy to create a prescriptive approach that works universally across all companies. But it is possible, as demonstrated in these pages, to identify successful practices of key business leaders, to custom-fit these best practices to your current operations, and to focus your company on those critical capabilities that will position your business for the twenty-first century marketplace.

If you take anything away from this book, it should be this: Leaders who practice ruthless execution principles and practices are best positioned to pull themselves through various setbacks and capture future growth opportunities.

You've been given a great deal of information to process in these pages. A key point to remember is that there is a logical sequence to the various strategies elaborated on and a set of common themes that link all of these strategies together.

As noted in Chapter 1, "Introduction to Ruthless Execution," business leaders who have successfully broken through the wall progress through a sequence that roughly follows the order of this book:

- Recalibrate your strategies (leadership).
- Recalibrate your business (critical capabilities).
- Recalibrate your rules (governance).

The very first step that business leaders should take in becoming "ruthless" is to recalibrate their business strategies and put into action a periodic strategic review and refinement process. They must then ensure that the business has addressed the critical capabilities required to compete in today's business environment, including maintaining a relentless focus on its customers' success while identifying cloud-enabled business opportunities. After having defined these core strategic intentions, leadership should review and realign the business portfolio of business initiatives, assess how resources are being allocated to various initiatives, and hold the execution teams accountable for quarterly results.

Setting a new strategic course requires strong analytical capabilities. It requires carefully, but swiftly, examining strategic options in a rigorous and thorough manner, and learning what truly matters in the marketplace.

Next, having learned what it is they want to do, business leaders must figure out how to do it. In effect, they need to recalibrate key governance elements and establish new rules of the game. They must establish processes that drive accountability and discipline to focus on what matters. To that end, there should be a clear focus on results, because that is the only thing that matters to these leaders. The system they put in place emphasizes that. Explaining away unfavorable results is not an option for them.

We strongly advise following the aforementioned logical sequence. In other words, it makes more sense to recalibrate various strategies *before* attempting to establish the rules of the game, and it makes more sense to establish your critical capability opportunities *before* recalibrating execution.

This is not to say that you must begin governance-like activity only after you have recalibrated various strategies. Certainly these strategies can and often do occur at the same time. It is, however, difficult and less effective to focus on the next step without having a strong base from which to work.

The bottom line is that business leaders need not change what they are about and need not alter their personalities. Rather, they must change what they do and what they focus on. The business leaders highlighted in this book have various personas. Some are great public speakers, outwardly forceful and aggressive; others are more laid back, shy, and retiring types. Indeed, the leadership ingredients required to break through any wall are divorced from such personality traits. Those ingredients simply require business leaders to be profoundly objective and straightforward and to deal with a company's options, the rules of the game, and the required actions. The point here is that all leaders and change agents can benefit from adopting these leadership ingredients, whether they are leaders of a business, functional area, or any organization.

One final thought: You will by now have realized that this book has addressed one of the profound business issues of today—how to effect change within an organization. The book talks about a particular kind of change, one that is required of business leaders to effectively navigate through business reversals. To manage through such times, these leaders have to effectively navigate through performance uncertainties to change the core business practices of their companies. This book provides a roadmap for doing just that.

Even at this late stage of the book, you may be asking, How can I know whether my company, more than other companies, needs to pursue these prescriptions? Simply ask yourself whether your organization has been underperforming relative to its peer group for a significant period of time (at least one year) or if you believe you are not best positioned for future success in your industry or marketplace; then ask yourself whether your organization has tried to close these performance gaps with little or no material impact. If the answer to either of these questions is "Yes," you have every reason to believe that you will benefit by putting the ideas behind *Ruthless Execution* into practice.

As mentioned throughout the book, all companies go through ups and downs and typically will experience performance plateaus or even hitting the wall on more than one occasion. *Unfortunately, most transformation efforts start fast but can peter out over time,* usually within the first two years. It is at this point that most companies find themselves going through the motions and complacency sets in. These companies may continue to measure their transformation "activities," but they are no longer measuring for results that matter. They are on autopilot. It is imperative that you are always keeping an eye out for the signals and perform reassessment on a regular basis. The practices we talk about in this book must become part of the corporate DNA and not merely one-time events.

This book has laid out numerous practices that are key to breaking through the wall (for example, the STAR process integrated with a quarterly portfolio management discipline). To break through a wall, it's not necessary to employ every single one of these practices. It's really up to you to pick and choose which of these seem the most appropriate as you wrestle with your own specific set of business dilemmas.

The question remains: How can you figure out which of these strategies to use?

To help you with that, we have developed a Ruthless Execution Index. It is a list of statements to help gauge the extent to which your organization ruthlessly executes. These statements offer "signposts," or if you will, "red flags," that you need to watch out for in your business.

Ruthless Execution Index (Spreadsheet)

Here are the instructions for using the Ruthless Execution Index:

1. In Table 13-1, you will find 54 statements on the left side of the Index.

2. Go through the list of statements and circle the number that best corresponds to your level of agreement with each statement (Disagree = 0; Somewhat agree = 1; Strongly agree = 2).

3. Add up the numbers:
   - If you score between 0 and 35, you are far from ruthless execution and have significant risks in your organization.
   - If you score between 35 and 72, you have good execution practices, but have some gaps to close.
   - If you score above 72, you are ruthlessly executing.

Table 13-1 Ruthless Execution Index

Statements	Disagree	Somewhat Agree	Strongly Agree
Leadership			
1 My company clearly understands which customers are most profitable and why.	0	1	2
2 We have detailed knowledge of what creates value for our customers.	0	1	2
3 We know what share of that value we capture.	0	1	2
4 Our company is relentless about ensuring a direct linkage of initiatives to strategic imperatives.	0	1	2
5 Our company's key "battlefields" are clearly communicated and well understood across the organization.	0	1	2
6 We are spending the right amount in the right areas.	0	1	2
7 Our company effectively balances between short-term performance and longer-term growth investments.	0	1	2
8 Our investment/project selection process requires business leaders to allocate total costs and benefits to their P&L statements.	0	1	2
9 We have a planning and review rhythm (quarterly milestones).	0	1	2
10 Our investment decisions are based on sound analytical rigor.	0	1	2
11 We effectively analyze and prioritize initiatives/investments.	0	1	2
12 Our company has a way of measuring its return on investment portfolio (return on strategy).	0	1	2

Statements	Disagree	Somewhat Agree	Strongly Agree
Leadership			
13 Our company has relationships with customers at the senior executive level and is viewed as a strategic partner.	0	1	2
14 Our leadership and board spend time understanding the value we deliver to customers.	0	1	2
15 Our leadership and board are intimately involved with our company's "cloudification" and Big Data strategy.	0	1	2
Critical Capabilities			
16 Our company effectively and regularly manages costs and productivity. It's in our DNA.	0	1	2
17 We have cost management institutionalized throughout the organization.	0	1	2
18 Our people understand and effectively manage working capital.	0	1	2
19 Our leadership and board are "IT smart."	0	1	2
20 Our IT investments clearly drive measurable value for the company.	0	1	2
21 Our cost performance is better than our peer group's.	0	1	2
22 We have a proactive and disciplined process for quantifying and communicating the value we deliver to customers.	0	1	2
23 Our company actively and consistently assesses opportunities for timely acquisitions and divestitures.	0	1	2

Statements		Disagree	Somewhat Agree	Strongly Agree
Critical Capabilities				
24	We have a formal plan and process to collect, analyze, and act on Big Data from our customers and products.	0	1	2
25	We have a process that requires and ensures that projects deliver on key milestones every three months.	0	1	2
26	We have investigated and implemented cloud-enabled business practices to impact our customers, suppliers, and competition.	0	1	2
27	We have the skills and capabilities to innovate our products and services through the cloud.	0	1	2
28	We have a formal process to collect, analyze, and act on customer experiences.	0	1	2
29	We regularly quantify and communicate the value we deliver to our customers.	0	1	2
30	Our company ensures that top talent gets allocated to strategic projects.	0	1	2
31	We are consistently developing talent at all levels of the organization.	0	1	2
32	Our leaders have deep succession plans.	0	1	2
33	Our senior leadership spends one day per week finding and developing new talent.	0	1	2
Governance				
34	We have across-the-board buy-in and compliance for investment selection criteria from all senior leadership.	0	1	2
35	The senior-most leaders of our company are actively involved in the prioritization and review of initiatives.	0	1	2

Statements	Disagree	Somewhat Agree	Strongly Agree
Governance			
36 We validate and measure our strategies in a rigorous and fact-based manner.	0	1	2
37 Our company clearly links incentives and rewards to results, not activities.	0	1	2
38 Our company regularly performs post-implementation audits of initiatives to assess actual costs and benefits.	0	1	2
39 Our company has good visibility into 90 percent of the projects and initiatives across the entire enterprise.	0	1	2
40 We have a diverse set of competencies on our board and senior leadership, including IT acumen.	0	1	2
41 Our company can easily address mid-term funding or reallocation requests when an appropriate opportunity presents itself.	0	1	2
42 Our company has established a common lexicon and set of standards by which investment decisions get made.	0	1	2
43 Our company has an effective method for identifying and funding cross-functional initiatives.	0	1	2
44 Our company has a high compliance rate as it relates to following decision-making standards.	0	1	2
45 Our company has a culture of discipline and rigor.	0	1	2
46 Our company has an effective process for allocating resources to strategic investments.	0	1	2

Statements	Disagree	Somewhat Agree	Strongly Agree
Governance			
47 Our company focuses on less than five performance measures by which results get judged.	0	1	2
48 We revisit and recalibrate our operating measures every two years.	0	1	2
49 Our company revisits and recalibrates its operating budget on a quarterly basis.	0	1	2
50 Performance measures are applied consistently and fairly across all investments.	0	1	2
51 Our company's performance measures are easily understood by the troops and are relevant to their daily activities.	0	1	2
52 Our company sets "stretch goals" that are fact based and defendable.	0	1	2
53 Our company has the technical tools to effectively prioritize investments and track performance.	0	1	2
54 We kill/close nonperforming initiatives on a regular basis.	0	1	2
Total Score:			

Index

U-V

W-X-Y-Z